ADVANCE PRAISE

"*Nikki embodies bold leadership, tenacity, and grit. This book reveals what's possible when you find your purpose and pursue it with lasting conviction.*"

—TRACEY DOI, CFO AND GROUP VICE
PRESIDENT OF TOYOTA NORTH AMERICA

"*In Beyond Barriers, Nikki encourages readers to level up and enthusiastically take on challenges for bigger and bolder dreams.*"

—KARA GOLDIN, FOUNDER AND CEO OF HINT®

"*In this book, Nikki encourages risk-taking, bold decision-making, and persistence in achieving personal and professional goals. A must-read for anyone looking to make their dreams a reality.*"

—RACHEL MICHELIN, CEO OF CALIFORNIA WOMEN LEAD

"*If you are a female entrepreneur looking for inspiration, Nikki will give you the courage you need to be a bolder you.*"

—VICKI SAUNDERS, FOUNDER AND CEO OF SHEEO

"Nikki's personal triumphs in the face of adversity and tireless pursuit of happiness remind us all to strive for a life that's not lived in black and white—but one that's lived in full color."

—BETH BROOKE-MARCINIAK, VICE CHAIR—
PUBLIC POLICY AT EY GLOBAL

"Every now and again, you meet an individual who transforms you. When in their presence, you awaken to a new level of being that makes the impossible possible. Nikki is that spark!"

—KARI WARBERG BLOCK, FOUNDER
AND CEO OF EARTHKIND

"In Beyond Barriers, Nikki teaches readers the all-too-important yet hard-to-recognize-in-the-moment lesson that when one door closes, another door opens. Her story of resilience and actionable takeaways make this a productive, inspiring read for anyone looking to level up in life—and aren't we all?"

—STEPHANIE KAPLAN LEWIS, COFOUNDER
AND CEO OF HER CAMPUS MEDIA

"Women entrepreneurs must dream bigger and go beyond barriers. Nikki knows that we can all overcome adversity and is an inspiration for her perseverance and resilience. She leads by example, living her purpose, turning obstacles into opportunities, and choosing happiness every day."

—PEGGY WALLACE, MANAGING PARTNER OF GOLDEN SEEDS

BEYOND BARRIERS

Dear Shona,

Here's to dreaming big, being bold and relentlessly going beyond barriers!

Much love,

Nikhi

BEYOND
Barriers

How to Unlock Your
LIMITLESS POTENTIAL

NIKKI BARUA

LIONCREST
PUBLISHING

BEYOND BARRIERS
How to Unlock Your Limitless Potential

ISBN   978-1-5445-1031-6 *Paperback*
       978-1-5445-1032-3 *Ebook*

To Mama and Papa, for inspiring me to dream big.

To Cheryl, for having faith in me through every failure.

To Monica, for filling my life with love, light and laughter.

Contents

Introduction

I first saw the pattern for a successful life while playing a video game. The game had captured my full attention as I furiously tried to get past the first level. Obstacles kept getting in the way, and my little video game character kept getting defeated and sent back to the starting point. But I didn't give up. I learned how to overcome the obstacles and defeat the various challenges along the way, and eventually, I reached the end. I was rewarded by getting sent to the second level to face harder challenges and bigger obstacles.

In a similar way, most of my life has been a series of peaks and valleys, up and downs. I would flourish for a while and do extraordinarily well, and then some major setback would occur and I would lose everything. I would suffer, struggle, and gradually build back up again. That was the pattern of my life for many years. The epiphany I had while playing the game radically changed my perspective on how I view obstacles and barriers. This shift in mindset began a process of evolution that has led me to where I am today.

A COLLAGE OF HEROES

When I was a little girl growing up in India, I had no fancy toys or Barbie dolls, and definitely no trips to Disneyland. I didn't grow up with access to global media or exposure to successful role models, but my father did something very special that left an imprint on my mind. He created a collage of pictures of inspiring women leaders and glued it to the inside of my closet door. At the center of that collage, he drew my face and wrote my name. That's it. He never said a word about it or explained what it was.

Every day I would open my closet door, look at the collage, and see myself surrounded by these role models. These courageous women were bold pioneers who weren't held back by any barriers. I grew up to believe that they were my friends, that I belonged among them, and that I could be just like them. I believed that I, too, had limitless potential to create extraordinary impact.

I did everything a good kid is supposed to do. I studied hard, I did my homework, I got good grades, and I was at the top of my class. I was a young overachiever, taking on more challenges than my peers, accomplishing incredible things, and making my family proud. However, I didn't feel like a hero—like the heroes in my collage. I felt lost and invisible. Perhaps I needed more interesting hobbies or cooler friends or more daring adventures. Perhaps I would be a hero if I simply went someplace else.

COMING TO AMERICA

As a young girl with big dreams, I believed America was the place where those dreams would come true, so in 1997, I set off for America to become a hero. My dream quickly turned into a nightmare. I felt homesick and isolated. I had few resources and little support, so I had to survive all kinds of challenges just to make it here.

Even the most mundane things felt unfamiliar and scary, like learning to use a washing machine; figuring out the difference between a penny, a nickel, and a dime; and learning to drive a car on the wrong side of the road. It seemed like everything I'd ever known was irrelevant now. To make matters worse, I felt different, like I didn't belong. Once again, I felt lost and invisible.

To survive, I did the only sensible thing I could think of: I imitated the people around me in the hope of fitting in. I embraced everything American, even working to get rid of my accent. I got a job at a big company, moved to a big city, and did my best to blend in. I blindly followed well-meaning advisors who said I must learn to play golf if I had any ambition to make it big. They told me I had to wear pantyhose and pearls to look the part and said I should follow sports so I could make small talk with clients. Well, I hate golf, I don't like wearing pantyhose, and I have zero interest in sports, but I did everything they said.

LOSING MYSELF, LOSING EVERYTHING

I did my job, I didn't break any rules, and I didn't challenge convention. I didn't talk about my journey as an immigrant. I didn't acknowledge my struggles as a person of color. I didn't complain about the opportunities I lost out on as a woman, and I certainly didn't tell anyone I was gay, not even my family. All I did was try to blend in. As I became more like everyone else, I became less like me. My world kept shrinking, and I felt more and more lost and invisible.

Years went by, and I continued to do more of what wasn't working. I had a carefully crafted persona: polished, professional, and picture perfect. Though I had a big social circle, I had no close friends I could count on. Though I lived a lavish lifestyle, I was buried in debt. I had a career filled with achievement, but I felt no fulfillment.

Then, in 2008, the market crashed, and my world fell apart. I lost everything I was afraid to lose. As if that wasn't hard enough, I also experienced the greatest hardship of my life when I lost my partner to suicide. In one week, I went from having a regular life to being depressed and broke. When you hit rock bottom, there aren't a lot of places to hide. I felt completely exposed. You have only yourself to lean on, and either you are strong enough to support yourself or you crumble under the pressure. I crumbled. I didn't have the will to carry on. I didn't want to get out of bed. I didn't even want to live.

That loss sent me into a very dark period in my life, a time filled with grief and pain. My personal tragedy felt overwhelming and paralyzing. I'd lost all sense of stability. A nothingness dropped over me, and all I could do was feel sorry for myself as endless questions went through my head:

Why did this happen to me? Why am I so unlucky? Why is it that, no matter how hard I try, I keep getting beaten down in my life?

DISCOVERING THE SECRET

Sometimes when we're in a dark place, we experience moments of real clarity that can illuminate the path to a better, more hopeful life. As these questions echoed in my mind, questions with no clear answers, I found myself one day playing a video game. I suddenly noticed something about the game. Everyone starts the game at level one. In order to get to level two, you first have to overcome the barriers of level one. To do that, you must understand the intricacies of that level, master the skills, and gain the competency, as well as develop the courage and conviction to keep going.

When you finally get to level two, you face even bigger challenges in order to get to level three. The competency you need now is even more demanding, the barriers bigger and more difficult. As you progress from level to level, you get stronger and better—even as the obstacles continue to get more difficult and the levels more complex. In that process, in the structure of the video game, I suddenly saw the pattern for a successful life.

Life presents many obstacles to overcome and infinite levels to conquer. Every level you conquer opens the path to bigger opportunity. The farther you go, the more you gain. But you have only a set amount of time to make progress. Once the timer runs out, you're done. The key to unlocking your limitless potential is to get as far as you can before your time runs out. The faster you scale those levels, the more impact you're able to create. To uncover all that is within your reach, you simply have to face life with the same optimism and determination as in that game as you move from level to level.

The secret to life's greatest treasures is to boldly face bigger and bigger obstacles. The more you embrace the struggle, develop the necessary skills and mindset, and build the courage and conviction to keep going, the more you succeed and thrive.

EVERY OBSTACLE CREATES OPPORTUNITY

Seeing that—really seeing it—gave me a brand-new perspective on my entire life. Suddenly, I could look back on my previous years like I was rewinding a movie and see everything I'd gone through, every painful circumstance, every heartbreak, every hardship. I realized that every difficult circumstance was an obstacle I'd overcome in order to progress. With every challenge, I'd catapulted forward, seized new opportunities that emerged, and developed greater confidence.

On the other hand, every time I found myself dealing with the same problems, I saw how I'd stunted my own growth and limited my own progress. Clearly, the times in my life where I'd been held back were times I had simply been stuck on the same level, waiting to learn the skills or acquire the courage to resume moving forward. In the parts of my life where I felt stuck, where I didn't feel like I was getting anywhere, I just needed to develop the right attitude, get the right perspective, and put in place the right systematic approach to get past that level.

YOUR PERSPECTIVE GIVES YOU POWER

This realization set me on a journey, growing and adapting to become the person I am today and guiding me toward who I want to be tomorrow. This epiphany in 2010 changed the course of my life. I marvel at how far I've come since my dark days when I was depressed, miserable, and broke. Until then, I'd experienced only moderate success in my career. I wasn't creating impact in any meaningful way.

Less than a decade later, I've built a multi-million-dollar business and earned recognition as a leading woman entrepreneur. I've launched an education platform that helps people develop their skillset and mindset for innovation. I'm an author and sought-after public speaker on bold leadership, diversity, and innovation, and I'm actively engaged in influencing public policy through nonprofit organizations. I was able to turn everything around, to open up and truly get on the path of unlocking my potential, because I changed the way I look at life.

We often overestimate what's possible in a year but underestimate what we can achieve in a decade. I've risen from the ashes, achieving success beyond what I thought was possible. More importantly, I've built a life focused on my purpose, living my true passion and being my authentic self. The game epitomizes the essence of how I perceive and approach everything. It has enabled me to achieve levels I never thought possible because I know now there is no end point. As long as the timer is running, I must keep forging ahead.

A FRAMEWORK FOR BOLDLY MOVING FORWARD

This change in perspective didn't make me fearless. I still worry about judgment and criticism. I feel all of the usual emotions when facing obstacles or hardships, but I now have a framework that empowers me to boldly move forward.

Before, it seemed like every year my problems got bigger and caused mounting distress. *Am I going to get through this?* I often wondered. Now I realize bigger challenges mean I'm at a higher level, which means bigger rewards. The problems I deal with this year will seem so much easier next year, just as the problem I dealt with last year seems so much easier now because of how much I've learned, developed, and grown.

That optimism encourages me constantly, and it gives me the creativity and resourcefulness that make it so much easier to find solutions. It doesn't guarantee I will solve every problem, nor does it ensure I will succeed every time, but even when I fail, I have a positive attitude that enables me to adapt and try again.

CLARITY, COURAGE, AND CONVICTION

In this book, I will present the framework that transformed my life. By sharing my own experience and the life experiences of other successful women, I hope to spur you into action. This framework is based on three pillars: clarity, courage, and conviction.

First, you need clarity about what you want to accomplish and why it matters. Just like in a video game, you won't continue trying to master a level if you don't care about it. The more you understand what you want and why it matters, the stronger your motivation will be to achieve it. Once you have clarity, you need the courage to move forward. That requires facing your fears head-on, planning for success, and flipping failure on its head. Finally, you need the conviction to persist—no matter how many setbacks you experience, no matter how many roadblocks you hit.

Everything becomes a learning experience when you have the right perspective. Instead of getting discouraged, you feel motivated to try different strategies, seek better tactics, and find the right solutions to overcome any barrier. You adapt. You celebrate how far you've already come. You keep moving forward, and you don't quit until you finally get past whatever barrier is in your way.

ADVENTURES OF BOLD PIONEERS

I learned this in my own life, but I initially wondered if it were, in fact, a universal principle. Will the strategies that took me from the lowest point in my life to the phenomenal success I'm now enjoying work for others? Are these ideas and philosophies coachable? These questions led me to study other successful people, to talk to them and hear their fascinating stories. I listened to the risk-taking adventures of bold pioneers—people who are obsessed with learning, growing, and achieving.

As I met these individuals, I asked each of them the same questions: *What led you to do what you do? What helped make you who you are? What enabled you to succeed?*

Even before I conducted any formal interviews, I talked to hundreds of successful people and noticed the same framework in story after story. I discovered that the essence of every success story is similar to what I had adopted in my own life. Every successful person has a compelling reason to pursue success, even if it isn't a glamorous reason. They have tremendous clarity and sharp focus about what they want to accomplish. Yes, they all have fears, but they don't let their fears hold them back or their failures stop them from trying again. Instead, they are relentless in the face of the future and have the tenacity to keep going, taking one step at a time—no matter what.

I found that successful people are all perpetual students. They are always learning, always studying the patterns of other successful people, and adapting as necessary. They have tremendous self-awareness and a hunger for feedback. They are creative and resourceful in overcoming challenges and are always willing to try new things. They all possess a keen sense of how far they've come, measuring their progress to fuel their enthusiasm and remain persistent.

For each person, there was a catalytic circumstance that led to their life choices. My own success story was born from personal tragedy. I had a compelling reason to find a way out of a dark place in my life. It took hitting rock bottom to experience my moment of clarity and see the path forward. The more I reflected on my own experience and learned from these inspiring people, the more I saw a pattern and the dots connected. That's how this framework emerged.

THE LIMITLESS POTENTIAL OF ORDINARY PEOPLE

So many people feel that success is elusive, that it's accessible only to the highly gifted, to people born with superior intellect, to people who went to top schools and landed the big jobs. They believe success comes only to those with powerful mentors or to those who are born into privilege and pedigree. When you approach life with those assumptions, you stunt your own potential. You shut off the possibilities before you, limiting yourself.

The people whose stories I share in this book are ordinary people, just like myself. I didn't come from privilege or pedigree. I'm not endowed with any special innate gifts. I have no extraordinary talents. Everything about my profile is ordinary, yet today, most people would consider me someone who has made an extraordinary impact. If I can do it, you can do it.

You have limitless potential and the opportunity to achieve

your dreams. All you need is the clarity to see it, the courage to pursue it, and the conviction to follow through step by step, level by level. You are limited only by the size of your dreams and your determination to get there.

This book isn't meant to be a "lean back and relax" reading experience where you just feel inspired by other people's stories. Instead, it's meant to combine inspiration with activation. The stories in this book allow you to see what's possible and apply the framework to your own life. When you see how the pieces connect, you will find a way forward.

EXERCISES

Each chapter contains a set of personal exercises intended to help you incorporate what you learn. These questions provide an opportunity for self-reflection, so answer them truthfully and without holding back. They are meant to build from chapter to chapter. By the end, the framework for your success will be in place, and we will have mapped your potential.

Are you ready for the next level? Let's go.

SECTION 1

CLARITY

People look everywhere to find the power they need to become the hero in their own story, but in reality, they need only to look within. By looking inward and connecting with yourself and your life experiences, you gain clarity on who you are. When you embrace that authenticity, you discover the true source of power, but in order to do that, you must understand who you are, what you want, and why you want it.

ELLEN'S STORY

Ellen Bennett is a twenty-nine-year-old entrepreneur who founded a very successful company called Hedley & Bennett, but her story really begins at nine years old, when her parents went through a bitter divorce. It was an ugly separation that left Ellen devastated, turning her whole world upside down. The shock of that tragic experience destroyed the ground beneath her so that she no longer knew who to count on or who to trust.

As a result, she decided she didn't want to depend on anyone but herself. She didn't want anyone to have the power to steal her sense of security ever again, so at a young age, Ellen made the decision to own her life. She would look out for herself and take every opportunity by the horns from that point on. That clarity has driven her ever since.

Ellen began to work at her mother's small apartment rental business. She crafted lease documents and other legal paperwork, paid bills, helped rent out apartments, and did any other work she could. Eager to gain independence and maturity, she learned everything she could and became very resourceful.

Overcoming Rejection with Tenacity

At the age of eighteen, Ellen moved from Los Angeles to Mexico City. She had absolutely no connection to the city, and her parents couldn't support her, but she did it anyway. She was completely on her own, and that was exactly what she wanted. Ellen took all kinds of odd jobs to support herself, overcoming rejection time and again and confronting many fears. For a while, she simply tried to survive. Over time, she learned how to promote herself, how to sell to people, and how to create influence. She also learned the power of courage, of never giving up in the face of hardship.

Ellen lived in Mexico City for four years and eventually achieved a modest amount of success. She attended culinary school, worked in a kitchen, and even bought a house. When her dreams starting getting bigger, she began to wonder what might be next in life. Those bigger dreams brought her back to Los Angeles at the age of twenty-two. She had graduated from culinary school by then, and she could have gotten a decent job in a thousand different restaurants in Los Angeles, but Ellen wanted to aim higher. She wanted to work for the best restaurant in town and be an apprentice to the best chef, so she went for it.

Ellen spoke to the hiring manager at Providence, one of the highest-rated restaurants in LA. She made a pitch for a job, and she refused to go away when they showed reluctance. Finally, impressed by her tenacity, they offered her a trial run over the course of a weekend. She took them up on the offer, but at the end of that hardworking weekend, they didn't offer her a job. Instead, they told her that they simply weren't hiring.

Even then, Ellen refused to give up. She kept contacting Providence periodically, pitching herself all over again each time. After much persistence, they offered her a position in the kitchen. She worked there for a year and a half, and because she was essentially earning minimum wage, she also worked at another restaurant, Baco, to make ends meet. She hung in there, learning and growing. Though Ellen didn't quite know what to do next, she knew she wanted to achieve something even bigger.

Everyone Deserves a Cape of Power

During her time at Providence and Baco, Ellen observed just how hard workers in restaurant kitchens have it, slogging away for long hours under intense pressure. She likened it to being an athlete enduring a long, grueling regimen every day. As she thought about the condition of these workers, she realized that part of what makes an athlete successful is looking like a champion. Ellen had recently signed up for a marathon, and when she did, she received a brand-new outfit from Nike. Putting it on, she admired the transformation. Now she truly looked like a champion, which boosted her enthusiasm for the race and actually contributed to her performance by making her feel better about herself.

Why don't people in restaurant kitchens have uniforms that make them look like champions? she wondered. *Super-heroes get awesome capes. Where is the cape of power for kitchen workers?*

This thought gave her the idea to design an apron that would inspire kitchen workers, making them look and feel like the champions and superheroes they are. She approached one of the restaurants where she worked and asked if they would consider ordering aprons from her, offering to create them faster and cheaper than their current supplier. All of that experience learning to sell effectively in Mexico City served her well—to her great delight, the restaurant took her up on the offer, and she got her first order for forty aprons.

Proactive Problem Solving

Ellen used the money from that first order to fund a brand-new business, Hedley & Bennett, acquiring the materials she needed to fulfill the order and hiring a skilled worker to sew the aprons. Unfortunately, the whole business almost derailed right away. She bought a roll of fabric for the uniforms, but the person making them screwed up the order. By that point, Ellen had already spent most of her money, so fixing the order was no easy feat. She could have felt sorry for herself, cried about the situation, or played the victim. Nobody would have blamed her.

Instead, Ellen went to work, getting proactive and creative to correct the problem. She went back to customers for input and refined the design throughout the process, so she wound up co-creating her core products with her customer base.

That first order was a success. More orders followed, and as workers responded positively, her reputation grew. Ellen is now five years into her business, supplying uniforms to 4,500 restaurants in the United States alone. Her company owns a 17,000-square-foot factory and sells to major stores across the country. Hedley & Bennett expanded their line of uniforms to include occupations beyond chefs and kitchen workers. Mario Batali and Martha Stewart are fans of her products, and her uniforms have been worn by staff at prestigious restaurants like Nobu and David Chang's Momofuku.

Ellen is a young, successful, millennial entrepreneur with a multi-million-dollar business, but success didn't come overnight. Looking back, she traces everything to that nine-year-old child of divorce, the child who decided to become independent, to never accept being a victim. She knew that if she couldn't count on anything else, she could count on herself. No matter what obstacles or barriers came her way, she always looked for a way to overcome them and keep moving forward. Ellen put herself in the driver's seat at all times, and she is flourishing in a male-dominated industry as a result.

AMY'S STORY

Amy grew up in a rural suburb of Knoxville, Tennessee, before becoming an entrepreneur based in the Bay Area. Amy's parents, like Ellen's, went through a traumatic divorce. The marriage fell apart when she was eight years old, but the bitter custody battle raged on for three more years. For Amy, the biggest trauma occurred when the court gave her the burden of selecting the custodial parent. She has never forgotten the moment when she sat in the judge's chambers, everyone listening as she made her decision, the court stenographer typing away.

Ultimately, she chose to live with her mom. That hurt her father deeply, of course, and Amy felt crushed about having to make the choice. She felt like she had rejected her father, and she grieved over the pain she had caused him. The experience of seeing her parents suffer over such a long period of time caused Amy to develop an extraordinary amount of empathy for other people. In fact, at times she has described it as a *debilitating* amount of empathy.

Driven by a Desire for Accomplishment and Understanding

When Amy turned thirteen, she began channeling her grief into self-improvement and extracurricular activities. She joined a cheerleading team, shed much of the weight she'd gained during the divorce, and threw all of her energy into academics and speech contests. Her success and public recognition in these areas were a welcome diversion from the lingering conflict between her parents and from feelings of guilt that came from disappointing them while trying to manage visitation schedules.

Amy continued her drive for accomplishment, exploring new things throughout high school and into college. She became valedictorian, enrolled at Vanderbilt, became the editor in chief of two publications, and developed a keen interest in exploring Japanese culture and language through an East Asian studies program. She learned to speak Japanese, studied abroad in Japan, and ultimately moved to Hokkaido for three years after college to fully immerse herself in the culture. Through these experiences, Amy developed even more empathy for cultural and human differences. She discovered a passion for understanding how people think, particularly those from backgrounds vastly different from her own, and continued to seek new experiences and friendships that would help her see different viewpoints.

Turning Debilitating Empathy into an Asset

When Amy returned to the United States, she landed a job with an online education startup and had the opportunity to watch executives make decisions about the website based primarily on what would be best for their business functions: engineering, marketing, publishing, and business development. However, no one focused on putting the customers' needs first. In this role, Amy discovered an opportunity to connect the dots from her past experiences, to be the voice of the customer at the table, to bring empathy for the user to business practices. She decided to conduct research directly with customers, socialized it with the company, and found her calling.

After the startup, Amy joined an early-stage UX (user design experience) software company, bringing user insights and empathy to Fortune 500 companies that were just starting to understand how to build digital products. Soon after, she launched her own UX research firm, which is now the go-to partner for innovative brands like Google, Amazon, and Facebook.

As Amy became a successful entrepreneur, her focus on promoting empathy in product design was the culmination of everything in her life—from the traumatic divorce of her parents, to the debilitating empathy she developed for her father and other people, to leveraging an intense drive for accomplishment, to her experience understanding other cultures. Amy created a way to transform millions of lives for the better through technology designed with empathy and inclusion in mind.

FINDING MY CLARITY

My own clarity came out of the darkest time in my life. Facing such massive personal loss sent me into a downward spiral. I had no motivation to do anything. I slept late, hated getting out of bed, and wondered how I would go about my day when I was constantly struggling and overwhelmed. I felt completely broken. My grief stopped being about my loss and became about the absence of identity and direction. Little did I know I was on the verge of my biggest breakthrough.

The real change happened one morning when I woke up, opened my eyes, and thought, *Today, I can make a choice. I can choose to be miserable, or I can choose to be happy.*

I chose the latter. I realized that happiness is a choice I

must make every day. The same is true of everyone. Every day, we choose whether or not we want to be happy. Happiness comes from hope. Hope comes from believing in something bigger than ourselves. For some, that bigger purpose is God, or family, or work, or community. For others, it's their dreams. People who are truly fulfilled, hopeful, and happy are committed to some great purpose that elevates them above their circumstances. That realization connected the dots for me, putting together the framework I had first begun to see while playing that video game.

FROM FEAR TO FREEDOM

I had been crushed with despair and hopelessness because I felt overwhelmed by the barriers in front of me. Now I realized the barriers were gifts that would allow me to strive for a bigger purpose. They laid out the path toward a higher level, toward greater fulfillment and success. Through these barriers, I could grow, learn, adapt, and achieve if I was willing to see them in a different light. Making the choice that morning brought about a sudden, profound shift in my life. It wasn't a slow transition. Once I made the choice, my mindset changed. Everything snapped into place. It was that dramatic.

I felt hopeful about the future and wondered about my

own bigger purpose. I recalled that collage from my childhood. I recalled that sense of optimism and belief that I was limitless, and I wondered why, despite all my successes, I had never felt limitless. Why did I feel so invisible? Why did I not feel like the heroes in that collage? My fear of not being accepted by others didn't allow me to accept myself. How could I possibly be a hero if I didn't embrace my whole self? How could I be limitless if I rejected so many parts of me?

For the first time, I asked myself, "Who am I?" And for the first time, I accepted the answer. I connected with myself, and suddenly a whole new world opened for me. You can't live your full potential if you don't embrace all of yourself. I had finally embraced my whole self. I became *unapologetically authentic*. That was my journey from fear to freedom.

BECOMING A CHANGE AGENT

Embracing myself allowed me to discover my purpose. I discovered that my purpose is to unlock people's potential, so I decided to dedicate the rest of my life to being a change agent who helps people transform. I had found that bigger purpose. I had clarity on who I am, what I want, and why that matters.

Now the challenge was figuring out how to live my purpose fully. How would I measure the impact? How would I create *massive* impact? *Could I impact a thousand lives? Ten thousand? Maybe I could reach a hundred thousand? How about a million?* In my hometown in India, a million people live in a single zip code. I wanted to touch even more lives, so I kept dreaming bigger and bigger.

A million felt challenging but reachable, but a billion people was absolutely scary, daunting, and impossible. That's why it was perfect. When you have a big, seemingly impossible goal, it unleashes your creativity and courage. If I were trying to reach only a thousand people, my approach would be radically different. I now had the purpose and goal that would propel me for the rest of my life.

SHIFTING MY FOCUS

Defining a big purpose gave my life meaning and lit me up. I had the clarity I needed to face the future with excitement, purpose, and direction, and that made everything fall into place. I stopped being inwardly focused, obsessed with my own pain and hardships. I started focusing on how I could help others.

I had always been achievement oriented, craving success in the traditional sense. In the past, my immediate goals might have been getting the next promotion, the next raise, the next car, or the next vacation. Now, I wanted to be successful so I could fund my big dream and change people's lives.

While my circumstances hadn't changed, my perspective had. Suddenly, I had a clear path forward. The gray lifted, and I could see where I needed to go, what I needed to be doing, and why it mattered. Once I gained clarity, I became an unstoppable force. I couldn't wait to start taking action.

THE HERO OF MY OWN STORY

I used to be a ghost, living in the shadows, hiding from my truth, but today I am standing in the spotlight. The more I embraced myself, the more I grew and transformed and inspired others. The collage from my childhood finally made sense to me: "Be the hero of your own story. Become the best version of yourself."

As human beings, we fear the unknown and the unfamiliar. We are wired to fear anything that's different from the norm. *But the differences in others help us grow. And the differences within us make us shine.* When you embrace your own authenticity, you go from living in the shadows to stepping into the light. You shed all the baggage that is keeping you trapped and hidden.

Authenticity makes you visible. Visibility creates awareness, and awareness leads to acceptance. You can't change hearts, minds, and attitudes if you are invisible. Authenticity is the key to unlocking your limitless potential. Embrace your personal power. Let authenticity be your activism.

WHAT OUR STORIES HAVE IN COMMON

What do Ellen, Amy, and I have in common? In all of our stories, some event helped us understand what we wanted and led us to discover who we truly are. Through hardship and adversity, we gained clarity about our own purposes and goals. Does that mean you must experience painful trauma to gain clarity? I don't think so. In later chapters, you'll find that the framework for success fits into all different kinds of lives—including your own.

In this section, we'll examine the three parts of clarity—knowing yourself, knowing what you want, and knowing why you want it—so you can begin to see the path that lies before you. Let's take the journey together.

CHAPTER 1

Know Yourself

It's so important to figure out your purpose in life because when you do, everything starts to feel effortless. Your purpose, after all, has to be more than simply working, paying bills, and surviving another day, right? You have gifts; you have skills and talents. Surely you are meant to do something meaningful with your life. Surely you are meant to fulfill some greater purpose.

Your purpose is born out of understanding yourself better. In order to figure out what you should devote yourself to, you must come to know who you are. In considering this question for my own life, I came to a realization: My greatest gift is seeing the gifts in other people. I have an innate ability to understand how people are wired, what makes them tick, what motivates them, and what holds them back. This ability allows me to help people unlock their fullest potential.

Much like the pioneers and change agents in the collage from my childhood, I resolved to become a pioneer without limits, a change agent serving the world around me. Once I realized my purpose and embraced it, I began to experience life at a different level. It changed the way I saw and approached everything.

HOW TO FIND YOUR PURPOSE

If you want to find your own purpose, figure out the one thing that comes most easily to you and brings you the most fulfillment. This is your gift, and it will provide the energy and enthusiasm you need to strive toward something bigger. When you don't enjoy what you do for a living, when you find it unfulfilling, it becomes almost impossible to sustain any momentum. The longer you waste time in unsatisfying work, the harder it becomes to feel any excitement about it.

Combining your gift with your passion is the key. Just like when you play a game, you'll never master something that you don't enjoy playing or that doesn't match your talents. You have to find the one game that is perfect for you, a game that holds your interest and benefits from your gift. When you begin to master that game, everything starts to feel effortless and fun. In the same way, your gift must be something you enjoy doing over and over again so you can reach the point where it feels effortless.

HOW TO KNOW YOURSELF

In this section, I will provide a set of guided questions to help you get to know yourself better. I have shared my own answers to these questions to help you think about how you might answer them for yourself.

Most people let their job or profession largely inform their identity. They typically introduce themselves by saying, "Hi, I'm So-and-So. I am the director of marketing at Such-and-Such Company." A name and a profession aren't the sum total of a person, but that's what our language often communicates.

We tend to think of ourselves as a living résumé, but how do you take an entire human being and shrink them down to one sheet of paper, defined simply by the schools they've graduated from or the jobs they've held?

If given the task to write an essay defining who they are, many people would struggle. It's not easy to become truly self-aware. The following questions are meant to help you gain more clarity on who you really are.

What Do You Aspire to Be?

What do you aspire to be? Who are your heroes? What are the three to five traits they all possess? What is the one word that describes your heroes? My heroes are the women leaders in that collage from my childhood. Each of them came from ordinary circumstances but created extraordinary impact in the world. My heroes are bold, visionary, pioneering, persistent, and purpose-driven.

The one phrase to describe my heroes would be "change agents." They weren't the richest or most famous, and none of them topped the list of people who have made the greatest impact on the world, but they all made a change to the world around them. That's exactly what I aspire to do.

What Do You Cherish?

What do you cherish? What achievements are you most proud of? In what ways are you like your heroes? How have your achievements given your life meaning? The achievements that I'm proudest of are those moments when I've positively impacted someone else's life, when

I've recognized the gift in another person and helped them unlock their potential. Seeing people thrive because I've helped unleash their true purpose fulfills me more than anything else.

That's when I feel the most like my heroes, because I know I've made a difference. Like my heroes, I am building a legacy by becoming a change agent for individuals and organizations.

What Is Your Identity?

What is your identity? Who are you? What is your purpose? What are your core values?

To answer the question of who I am, I look at both my heroes and my past achievements. My identity emerges from a combination of the two, which means the answer to the hardest question—who am I?—is fairly simple: I am a change agent. My mission is to unlock the limitless potential in as many people as I can, and my core values include courage, impact, and growth.

GET TO KNOW THE REAL YOU

When I framed my identity as a change agent with a mission to unlock the potential of a billion people, it opened up an entirely different worldview for me. It changed how I look at my life, my job, my connections, my relationships, and my location. This new vision provides an entirely different perspective for me.

No longer do I view myself as simply a job and a title. That limitation has been cast aside. I introduce myself with my new identity: "I'm Nikki Barua. I'm a change agent with a big mission to unlock the limitless potential of a billion people." I no longer allow the constraints of a limited self-image to hinder what I can achieve.

Now it's your turn. Think about these questions carefully and write down your answers. As you do so, you will transform the way you think about yourself. Your answers will provide clarity about who you really are and what you really do.

EMBRACE YOUR INNER SUPERHERO

In my self-examination, I looked to my heroes, the pioneers with a bigger purpose, the change agents. My heroes inspired me to embrace my inner superhero, even if it's a much bigger role than I had before.

When you aspire to something greater, it might seem impossible. You might not feel like you have the courage or readiness to step into the role. You might want to wait until you have acquired the skills or the resources you need. But there is no such thing as the perfect time.

Taking on a heroic persona can give you the courage and confidence you need to step into your dream. Think of it like Clark Kent transforming into Superman. As a regular person with a regular job and a regular life, he doesn't allow himself to enact the change he's fully capable of. But when he throws off the suit jacket, dons the cape, and embraces the superhero persona, suddenly he becomes daring and bold, capable of accomplishing the impossible and saving the day. The superhero persona helped me dream big, become unapologetically authentic, and lead a purpose-driven life.

I feel bold, daring, and resilient, but it's not the superhero persona that gave me these powers. The cape and costume didn't give Clark Kent his powers. In truth, he had those powers all along. The same is true of me. The boldness that I feel now was within me all along. What I'm doing is merely amplifying the traits I already have within myself.

Whether I realized it or not, I looked up to the women in the collage because I saw the same daring, tenacity, and grit in me. I saw the same kind of pioneer, the same bold leader, just waiting to be unleashed. It took time to recognize that I had the same attributes, but when I did, I realized I could achieve the same incredible things as they did.

YOUR IDENTITY SHAPES YOUR LIFE

Hopefully, the exercise has helped you better define who you are beyond your past or present circumstances, gaining clarity about who you want to be. Now it's time to become the hero of your own story by recognizing that you don't look up to your heroes just because they are extraordinary, but because you see yourself in them. You see the parts of yourself that you want to amplify, the parts you cherish most.

When you embrace that mindset, you begin to dream bigger. Your heroes become your peers, your equals, so you live, act, and dream just like them. My heroes never gave up. They showed tremendous resilience in the face of brutal adversity. If I'm like my heroes, and if I'm the hero of my own story, then I mustn't give up, either.

People act in congruence with the identity they adopt. If you think you're a champion, you will think and act like a champion. When you bring out the best in yourself, you discover the hero within you. Assume that identity, and everything in your life will align.

EXERCISE

1. What do you aspire to be?

....

   A. Who are your heroes?

   ....

   B. What are the three to five traits they all possess?

   ....

   C. What is the one word that describes your heroes?

   ....

2. What do you cherish?

....

   A. What achievements are you most proud of?

   ....

   B. In what ways are you like your heroes?

   ....

C. How have your achievements given your life meaning?

....

3. What is your identity?

....

A. Who are you?

....

B. What is your purpose?

....

C. What are your core values?

....

CHAPTER 2

Know What You Want

Everyone has a wish list—things to own, experiences to have, places to see—but unless you commit to making them come true, your wish list remains a fantasy. There's a distinct difference between "wishing" and "dreaming." Often, the things people wish for feel unattainable, but when people dream, there is a greater sense of desire. They fall in love with those dreams, and eventually those dreams start to feel real.

I have found that every achievement is preceded by a dream. When your dream connects with something that's meaningful to you, it creates intrinsic motivation that drives you toward your goals, but first, you must give yourself permission to dream. Some people feel like it's a futile exercise, so they hold themselves back. They try not to dream too big so they won't be disappointed. They stay within the realm of what they believe to be possible.

I believe we are gated by the size of our dreams, so we must dare to dream big. When you look back at some of the great achievements that have changed the world, they all seemed like crazy ideas at the time. These monumental feats didn't start with a clear roadmap and game plan of how they could be achieved. Instead, every breakthrough simply started as a dream that someone believed in, no matter how big or impossible it seemed.

Dreams create strong feelings of desire that propel you forward. Dreams are different from goals. Goals give us a sense of accomplishment when completed, but they aren't always motivating. Before you can establish a goal, you must want it, and you must know why you want it. You need a degree of emotional intensity, and dreams give us that intensity. If your goal stems from your dream, you will feel a constant drive pushing you toward it.

DREAM BIG

If your dreams are the pathway to your potential, and you are gated by the size of these dreams, then there's no reason not to dream big. In my experience, it takes the same amount of effort to achieve big dreams as it does small ones, so if you're going to dedicate yourself to achieving something, why not aim high?

You can't worry about how other people will react to your dream. Don't let anyone discourage you. Sometimes it feels foolish to aim high, so you might choose to limit your dreams. However, dreaming big unleashes your creativity to solve problems in very different ways than dreaming small, challenging you to achieve things that seem impossible.

When considering my mission to unlock the limitless potential in people, I didn't know how to make it measurable. A thousand people? A million? A billion? At the end of the day, did the number even matter? After all, nobody was forcing me to pursue this dream. Whether I set my goal at a million or a billion, neither of them were going to be easy. Each would take significant effort to achieve.

UNLEASHING MY CREATIVITY

How I would approach a goal of a billion people would be very different from how I would approach a goal of a million, or ten thousand, or a hundred. I knew touching a billion lives couldn't be done one person at a time, so I brainstormed different ways to reach more people. I defined five strategies that would give me leverage to create impact at scale:

- Build a business that transforms big corporations and positively affects their employees and customers.
- Create an education platform to empower people with strategies and solutions for personal and professional success.
- Become a public speaker to share my ideas with large audiences around the world.
- Write books to express my vision to and inspire action in a mass market of readers.
- Influence public policy in a way that would improve lives and create social impact.

If my dreams had been smaller, the solutions I came up with would have been radically different. The strategies I defined helped me move from an impossible dream to an actionable roadmap. Instead of feeling paralyzed by inertia, I could see the path forward. I was excited about the possibilities, no matter how challenging they seemed. That excitement propelled me toward my dream and made me strive harder. When you dare to dream big, you inevitably begin moving toward those dreams.

DREAMS DETERMINE YOUR OUTCOMES

I have done this exercise with many people, challenging them to make their dreams bigger and bigger until they seem impossible. When we first think of something we want, we're typically operating within the limits of our own mind. We dream about things that seem both rational and possible. That's why we must push beyond that horizon.

When we don't push ourselves to dream big, we limit the possibilities in our own lives. My conversation with a young woman about dreaming big brought to light how she had shut off bigger outcomes.

I asked her, "What's your biggest dream?"

She gave me a very precise answer. She wanted $237,000.

Curious, I asked, "Why that specific amount?"

"I want to help my mother," she replied. "My mother has $37,000 worth of debt that I want to help pay off. Also, she has always wanted to buy a house but could never afford one. It will be about $200,000 for the down payment and other expenses. If I could get that much money, I would be able to help my mom own a home and live debt free."

"Well, what if you could have more? Let's say I was a genie and I offered to make any dream come true. You could have anything you want. What would it be?"

She seemed uncomfortable with this line of questioning, so I told her to take a moment to think about it. Finally, she came up with a higher number.

"I would ask for $300,000."

"Why $300,000?" I asked.

"Well," she said, "with that much money, I could take care of my mom and pay off the balance on my student loans."

"What else could you wish for?" I asked. "What else do you want?"

I made her do the exercise again.

This time, she said, "You know what? I want a million dollars. It makes me uncomfortable to say it, but I think with that much, my mom would be taken care of and I'd have a nice place for myself. I would be able to take care of another family member who's been struggling. Plus, I could take my family on vacation and even put a good amount in savings."

"How would you feel if your dreams came true?" I asked.

Her eyes lit up. "It would completely change my life. It would help me take care of my mom, who has done so much for me in my life. It would enable me to support my relatives, who helped me get through school. It would allow me to pursue what I love instead of trading my life for a paycheck doing something I hate."

"How do you think you might go about activating your dream?"

When she first mentioned $237,000, she had no idea how to get the money. At the time, she was making a salary of $60,000, and she could barely afford to pay all of her bills. Trying to figure out how to make $237,000 in her job completely paralyzed her.

However, when presented with the challenge of making a million dollars, she immediately brimmed with ideas. She said she could start a business. She had ideas about ways to create value for other people. She didn't hesitate to jump all in to pursue her dream.

Watching this transformation happen in the span of half an hour fascinated me. I watched someone with an ordinary income and no defined dream go through an exercise that led to a very big dream, boosted her confidence, and energized her to make it happen.

At the end of the day, the number isn't what matters. The reasons behind that number are what matter. She wanted to help her mother and maybe provide a little bit for herself as well. That's what motivated and fulfilled her. Once she got excited about that idea, her creativity was unleashed, and she was able to truly dream. She began to see a whole new picture of what was possible.

Her newfound determination allowed her to look back and wonder why she had ever fixated on $237,000. Why had she thought so small when she could have so much more in her life? That's the power of dreaming big and not assuming your own limitations.

As the hero of your own story, what is your dream? My dream was to become a change agent who helps many people unlock their potential. Now let's dream bigger. What is that bigger dream? I decided I wanted to help a million people unlock their potential. Let's dream even bigger. What is an even bigger dream? I finally settled on a goal of reaching a billion people.

Now that you've identified your bigger dream, ask yourself why that dream is important to you. How would your life change if that dream came true?

GIVE YOURSELF PERMISSION TO DREAM BIG

Many books will tell you that if you just imagine your dream coming true, it will magically happen. That's not what I'm saying. Instead, I'm encouraging you to give yourself permission to dream big. When you do that, and when you're very clear about why it's important to you, you create the motivation you need to take the right actions to make that dream possible.

Tap into your own emotional intensity. Allow yourself to feel excited, and let that feeling spur you on. Every dream that I've documented in my journal seemed far-fetched and unachievable in the beginning. But it allowed me to identify what I want and why it's important to me so I can feel the excitement I need to get motivated. It unlocks the creativity that helps me make these impossible dreams possible.

We are all gated by the size of our dreams, so if you truly want to be limitless, you have to dream big.

XERCISE

1. As the hero of your own story, what is your dream?

   ....

2. Now dream bigger. What is that bigger dream?

   ....

3. Now dream even bigger. What is an even bigger dream?

   ....

4. Why is that dream important to you?

   ....

5. How would your life change if that dream came true?

   ....

CHAPTER 3

Know Why You Want It

You know what you want, but do you know why you want it? To make your dreams a reality, you have to take active ownership of them, and the only way to do that is by figuring out exactly why your dream is important to you. The "why" becomes your fuel to achieve your dream—the source of your intrinsic motivation.

For example, let's say you dream of owning a home. Why do you want to own a home? How does owning a home make you feel, and why is that feeling important? Questions like these help you gain clarity on the true reasons for your desire. Once you have clarity on the "why," you become focused and determined.

BENEFITS AND CONSEQUENCES

Let's suppose you've dreamed of owning a beautiful seaside villa since you were a little kid. You thought about it all the time as you were growing up, but now as an adult, you've given up on that possibility and live in a small rental apartment. How did that happen?

Somewhere along the way, the benefits and consequences of achieving that dream didn't make it worth striving for. You didn't have a "why" that was big enough. The benefits weren't significant enough. The consequences weren't intolerable enough. Your life was just fine even if you didn't own that seaside villa.

For any dream to come true, you need a clear reason to pursue it. Either the benefits are meaningful and exciting, or the consequences of not realizing your dream are unacceptable. Only under those conditions will you find strong enough motivation to reach for the impossible.

CLARITY TO OVERCOME BARRIERS

People who successfully achieve their dreams realize that the path to get there is fraught with barriers, and they embrace the adversity. Those who fail to realize their dreams don't expect the barriers, don't know what to do about them, and eventually give up.

When people are clear about what they want and why they want it, they are able to push through every obstacle. They don't focus on the "what," and they don't get stuck on the "how." They stayed focused on the "why."

During my journey, the "how" of my dream changed many times. I tried different approaches. Some worked, and others didn't. I've pivoted multiple times and adapted my methods, but the "why" has always remained clear, creating a powerful guide that has allowed me to overcome every barrier I've encountered and stay focused on my ultimate desired outcome.

DISCOVERING YOUR "WHY"

Maybe you're unsure of the "why" behind your big dream, and you don't know how to go about figuring it out. Follow the exercises at the end of this chapter to gain clarity and discover your "why."

Your big dream, the one that you've been cultivating, that you have expanded upon over the years, the dream that feels almost real to you—take that dream and visualize it in some way. Create an illustration that will bring it to life for you. In my case, I compiled magazine covers, pictures, quotes, and headlines that inspired me. This created a visual representation of my dream and made it feel real and achievable.

After you have visualized your dream, create a list of the benefits and consequences associated with that dream. The bigger your list, the more clarity you will achieve. I chose to describe the ten most positive things I would gain if my dream came to life and the ten most unacceptable consequences if I abandoned the dream.

When you have your list, evaluate how willing you are to avoid the consequences and reap the benefits. Would you be satisfied living without some of the benefits? Could you settle for some of the consequences? Are the benefits significant enough that you refuse to settle for less? Are the consequences of failing to achieve your dream intolerable?

Think about what you want to achieve and how far you want to go. Once you have that dream, work to understand the reason behind it, the "why" that has put this dream in your heart. Weigh the benefits of realizing your dream and the consequences of failing to achieve it. All of these things together will create the motivation you need to go beyond wishful thinking to reach the outcome you desire.

DISCOVERING MY "WHY"

In my self-examination, I had to consider the benefits of reaching a billion people. If I could get the same benefits from impacting a billion lives as I would from impacting ten thousand, then why would I even bother trying to reach a billion? If the benefits were the same, I would settle for the lesser dream. You have to answer this question for yourself. Would you obtain greater benefits by pursuing a bigger dream? Are those greater benefits impossible with a smaller goal?

Motivation comes not only from the possibility of reward but also from a desire to avoid pain. Your level of commitment derives not only from your desire to gain the benefits but also from a desire to avoid the consequences. These two things create the ceiling and the floor of your dream. Figure out what that looks like for you, and that will determine how far you're willing to go to achieve your dream.

My dream of unlocking the potential of a billion people came from hitting rock bottom and not wanting to live any more. I had lost hope and given up on myself, and I never wanted anyone else to do the same. The consequences of not pursuing my dream felt intolerable. My sense of survival didn't allow me to descend into that place. Changing my life would change the lives of so many others. I wanted to become a catalyst who could create hope in other people.

In turn, my desire to ignite change in others actually

changed me. I found myself fundamentally transformed as a person by taking this journey, because the effort required me to become bolder and more daring. I had to put myself in the public realm. I had to become an entrepreneur. All of this required me to learn new skills and reach new heights. If I achieve my mission of reaching a billion people, the broad benefits for society will be significant, but the personal benefit to me will be the unlocking of my own limitless potential.

I will have built a great company that transforms large organizations, empowers their employees, and helps their customers live better lives. I will have unlocked the potential in people through my education platform, which is designed to transform personal and professional lives. I will have inspired people as a speaker and an author. I will have shaped public policy designed to create social impact. Through all of these actions, I will have unlocked people's potential—and also unlocked my own.

EXERCISE

1. What will you achieve if your dream comes true?

    ....

2. What are the benefits if you achieve your dream?

    ....

3. What are the consequences if you don't pursue your dream?

    ....

4. Are the benefits significant enough for you to not settle for less?

    ....

5. Are the consequences intolerable enough for you to not settle for less?

    ....

SECTION 2

COURAGE

Fear comes from our belief that something painful is likely to occur. We have a natural instinct to avoid pain, so we succumb to fear and become too paralyzed to take action. On the other hand, courageous acts are born out of faith and confidence. Faith comes from our belief that something positive is likely to occur. Faith leads people to go beyond their limitations and past their fears. Both fear and faith emerge from our beliefs, but fear produces despair, while faith gives us hope. Courageous people aren't fearless. They simply have more faith than fear.

NOHA'S STORY

Noha Waibsnaider, founder of Peeled Snacks, was born

in Israel and spent her early childhood there. When she was four, her father started showing signs of mental illness. Her mother suggested the family move to her native Argentina in the hope that leaving the conflict in the Middle East would improve his mental health. As Noha's father, formerly a successful economist, lost his hold on reality, everything changed for the family. He could no longer work in his chosen profession, so he wound up earning a much smaller income selling fruits and vegetables at a local market.

Noha's family struggled to make ends meet, and ultimately, her father's worsening condition tore the family apart. He was diagnosed with schizophrenia, and in the confusion of his illness, he demanded a divorce from Noha's mother. Distraught by the loss of her husband, Noha's mother decided to distance her daughters from the disease and immigrated to the United States. They had to adjust to a new country all over again and faced many hardships as undocumented immigrants. Noha's life was marked by instability and insecurity. She moved from house to house, ultimately living in thirteen different places in three countries by her fourteenth birthday.

Learning to Adapt

The constant changes, insecurity, and adversity of Noha's

early life taught her to roll with the punches. Noha developed a passionate interest in mental health, and as she looked for contributing factors, she began to focus on how nutrition might have an effect. This obsession evolved into a broader recognition of how food affects our quality of life and well-being.

Eventually, this passion inspired an entrepreneurial idea. In 2004, Noha launched her own company, Peeled Snacks, which makes organic dried fruit snacks without added sugar or preservatives—a healthy alternative to traditional snack foods. The company later expanded to veggie snacks, with pea-based savory puffs that provide protein and fiber. Peeled Snacks' mission sounded simple—to increase people's access to healthy food and make them feel good about snacking—but simple things aren't always easy.

Digging a Tunnel with a Spoon

The company launched long before a major market for organic, healthy food existed, so it had an unproven business model. At that time, the food industry lacked capital for early-stage companies, and Noha couldn't find willing investors to fund her endeavor. She turned to friends and family for help, but ultimately, she had to use whatever resources she could find just to get the business off the ground. As she describes it, she felt like she was digging a tunnel with a spoon.

Despite the adversity that came from being first in her market and trying to prove the viability of a new product, Noha worked relentlessly. She adapted and navigated through difficult times, including a major setback that occurred when a worldwide mango crop failure left the company with a dire shortage of their number one product for almost a year. In the most difficult moments, she chose to take courageous action because Peeled Snacks was about more than creating a successful business. Noha wasn't simply trying to sell a product. She was advocating for better nutrition, trying to change the way people eat, and building a movement with a clear mission of improving lives, health, and well-being.

Noha pioneered this space, and her company succeeded as a result. Peeled Snacks still leads in the health food marketplace with distribution in all major retail stores across the country. She continues to use her business and brand as a platform to advocate for better nutrition.

Giving Up or Getting Inspired

Noha's story illustrates the choices people make after going through extraordinary adversity. When faced with difficult circumstances, a person can react in one of two ways: give up and become hopeless, or use the adversity as inspiration.

Her experiences moving to different countries and adapting to different languages and cultures enabled her to adapt to new situations faster and more easily than most people—a significant advantage when pioneering in business. Her father's struggle with mental illness fueled her mission of advocating better nutrition for improved mental and physical health.

She led the way with a business idea that didn't have much initial support, but instead of becoming discouraged and choosing something easier, she stuck with her vision. She built an authentic brand that has become the best-known brand in its category. Above all, she transformed herself and achieved her dream through courageous action and perseverance.

JANE'S STORY

Jane Barratt, founder and CEO of GoldBean, a financial services and technology company, was born in Melbourne, Australia, one of eight kids from a large family. Her father held numerous blue-collar jobs, yet he managed his money well. As a result, the family thrived. He even managed to afford private school education for all of the children. Jane's mother didn't simply want to raise eight kids; she wanted to raise eight confident individuals. She encouraged them to embrace their own unique personalities and find their own paths.

"You can do anything you want in life," she often said, "as long as you figure out how to pay for it yourself."

As a child, Jane became obsessed with television commercials. She found them more entertaining than the regular programming, and given her limited exposure to the white-collar world, advertising seemed like a great career, a place where she could bring her storytelling abilities to life.

When she was only eleven years old, Jane set a goal to someday run a Madison Avenue advertising agency. The circuitous route she took to get there enabled her to fulfill this dream before the age of forty. Jane credits an early career decision to work in Asia as the key to fast-tracking her success. The transition created a huge cultural shift for her, but like Noha, Jane adapted to the change.

Driven by a Dream
Ultimately, her dream of having adventures in life and

business was helped by many mentors along the way. During her time in Asia, a number of powerful women instilled in her a sense of focus and a no-nonsense approach to leadership. This proved extremely useful when she became a manager, helping her handle serious situations, including an outbreak of the SARS pandemic in her office building, multiple market downturns, and the dot-com crash that wiped out so much of the burgeoning digital space.

Throughout her career, a positive mindset kept her learning and growing. She rose to meet each new challenge, and the confidence she built informed her entire journey. One thing she did to cultivate her mind was to keep an idea journal. Anytime she came up with an interesting idea, she wrote it in the journal so she could spend time contemplating it. If, after a time of contemplation, it seemed like a good idea, she took action. If an idea failed, she just chalked it up to a learning experience and tried something else.

After her children were born, she put the journal in storage. Ten years later, she pulled it out again and was amazed to discover that one of the ideas she'd written was for a technology platform that would allow people with limited resources to invest. This idea became her company, GoldBean.

Fulfilling Her "Why"

In all of this, Jane's "why" came from an insatiable curiosity about people and the world, a fascination with the broader economy and how companies work. This culminated in the creation of a company that not only gave her a better life but also helped others do the same thing. Jane's company provides a platform for people of limited means to become savvy investors and share in the economy that they are driving. Jane would not have gotten this far if she hadn't achieved her goals early in life. This allowed her to gain clarity on what she wanted, why it mattered to her, and how she could take more risks in life.

Starting GoldBean required tremendous courage. Operating a business in New York City is difficult enough, but competing in the overlap of the financial services and technology fields (FinTech) proved even more challenging. It's an extremely male-dominated and monocultural industry, but Jane proved a rarity. She has become one of the few women to build her own FinTech company from scratch.

She recognized that by taking risks and taking action, she would learn from setbacks and gain confidence from her successes. Through it all, she maintained her faith in a better future, living by the motto "Next year will be bigger."

Jane, Noha, and countless other pioneers have achieved

success through courage. They faced their fears, learned from their failures, grew confident in their successes, and moved confidently in the direction of their dreams.

BEING COURAGEOUS

In any circumstance, you can choose to be driven by either faith or fear. If you choose faith, you will continue moving forward. It breaks down the barriers created by fear. Since fear is imaginary, it gains power when you let it become a big, scary thing in your mind because you desperately avoid dealing with it. With the change in perspective brought on by faith, you can demystify your fear, evaluating it and breaking it into more manageable pieces.

Once you break down fear into smaller pieces, you can begin to understand where it comes from and what it's made of. That enables you to start taking action. As you experience success, you gain confidence and develop deeper faith, causing your fear to diminish even further. When you start to move boldly forward, even failure can't overwhelm you because you believe you can recover from any setback. That's why courage is not about being fearless but moving forward despite fear.

CHAPTER 4

Face Your Fears

Fear is designed to help you survive by motivating you to protect yourself from danger. However, fear is also selfish because when you feel fear, you mostly think about your own needs. Your mind goes into survival mode. When you live in fear, it's almost impossible to focus on helping others. Even when you fear losing a loved one, the feeling is ultimately selfish because you're focused on someone being taken from you. You can't step outside of yourself; you can't see things from anyone else's perspective. You feel trapped.

FEAR IS SELFISH

We are all limitless, possessing a wealth of gifts and abilities. When we unleash our gifts, we create impact in the world, but fear holds us back. Fear creates a wall that prevents us from bestowing those gifts on others, and it also blocks what we might receive in return. If you can get past that barrier, you can give your gifts to the world, and it's in giving that you find a better life. When you give, you get.

If you want to make a difference in the world, you have to get past fear and see beyond your own survival. Otherwise, you're in danger of becoming stuck in survival mode. True success in life comes from creating more value for others. You can see this at many levels. For example, if you want to grow your business, give more value to your customers. If you want a more loving relationship with your spouse, give more love than you expect to get back.

Success is a return on the investment you make in other people. The more you give, the more you get back, but you can't operate this way when you're stuck in survival mode and operating from a place of fear. You have to learn to coexist with fear and not allow it to control you. Don't avoid fear. Face your fear and take action anyway. When you do this, you will experience a tremendous amount of uncertainty and discomfort, but you will also learn and grow. Your creativity will be unleashed, and you will find a way through your struggles.

HOW I DEFEATED FEAR

When I first developed my big dream, I thought, *This seems unachievable. How do I even begin to pursue it?* Faced with this daunting task, I decided not to tell anyone about it. If no one knew about my big, audacious dream, then no one would make fun of me for failing to achieve it.

However, I knew that this line of thinking was merely an excuse to avoid taking action. My fear of failure held me back. Once I realized this, I decided to face it. I made a list of all my fears. That list grew to twenty-seven distinct fears ranging from the rational to the completely irrational.

I rated all twenty-seven fears and found that the majority of them were unfounded and based on poor assumptions. The worst-case scenario proved much less severe than I'd imagined.

Some of those fears had already come to pass. For example, I'd made it through severe financial hardship and come out the other side. If I could survive it once, I could survive it again. The positive outcomes of getting past my fears were so tremendous that even if I failed miserably, I would still be further ahead in the process.

EACH TIME I FAIL, I GAIN A LITTLE MORE

Just like in the video game, each time I fail, I gain a little more skill, a little more knowledge, and a little more determination to reach the goal. Once I faced that whole list of fears, they lost their potency. They no longer had a hold over me. Almost immediately upon completing the exercise, I felt propelled into action.

Through the exercise, I also turned what had seemed like innumerable fears into a manageable list. What had felt like a vast mountain before me became a relatively small number of named fears, and out of those twenty-seven, most of them proved to be unfounded. The remaining fears on the list still seemed real, but I had already faced some of them, so I knew I could face them again.

In the end, I was left with only a couple of fears that seemed real and that I hadn't yet experienced. However, when I thought through them, I realized the positive outcomes of those fears outweighed the negative, which made the risk well worth it. Suddenly, I had no more excuses for letting fear hold me back.

Your fears might still stand like a wall in front of you. It's time to confront them, to see them for what they really are, so you can move past them. Don't let them hold you back any longer. Your limitless potential is waiting.

FACING YOUR FEARS

Here's an exercise that can help you face your fears.

First, identify all of the fears associated with pursuing your dream. When you first discover your big dream, you get super excited about it because you've found something that motivates you. Shortly after defining this dream, however, you hit a wall. Fear associated with that dream rises in front of you. To get past that wall, you have to identify these fears. What is it about pursuing your dream that scares you? Write these things down so you can see them. My list included fears ranging from a fear of failure to a fear of judgment, even a fear of success.

Second, measure the magnitude of each fear. Give them each a number on a scale from one to ten. This helps you determine which of your fears have the biggest hold over you. Once I rated each of my fears, I discovered that I had only a handful of fears that rated high.

Third, go through the list and create a worst-case scenario for each fear. What's the worst that would happen if each of these fears came to pass? I learned that the worst-case scenario for each of my fears was not as bad as I had imagined, and in most cases, I came up with a solution to overcome that potential adversity. In fact, only a few of my worst-case scenarios were truly debilitating.

Fourth, go through the list again, but this time consider a positive outcome that could result if each of these fears came to pass. It might seem odd to think about positive things coming from your worst fears, but this part is crucial in helping you overcome them. Sometimes, by examining our fears from a different perspective, we realize that they aren't as bad as we thought, and that some good might even come from them. The positive outcomes of overcoming my fears proved to be much greater than the negative impact of the fears themselves. For example, if I launched a business and it failed, the experience of becoming an entrepreneur would enable me to try again.

Suppose you have an idea for some big innovation at your job, but in order to attempt it, you have to take a risk that could get you fired. You fear your boss might be furious if he finds out what you're attempting to do. That's a considerable fear, so you rate it a six on your list.

What's the worst-case scenario for that fear? Obviously, becoming unemployed. However, the reason you lost the job would have value. Now you can position yourself as an innovator and a risk-taker. You have shown the world that you are bold and courageous in the face of fear. What positive outcome might result? Doors of opportunity might open for you. In fact, after losing the job, you might realize that working there wasn't right for you, that it didn't make you happy, and that you're better off pursuing some other job.

Finally, think about how the hero in your story would face these fears. Would the hero take courage and confront fear? Of course. If you want to become the hero of your own story, begin doing the same.

EXERCISE

1. What are your fears in pursuing your dream?

   ....

2. What is the magnitude of each fear on a scale of one to ten?

   ....

3. What is the worst-case scenario for each fear?

   ....

4. What is the positive outcome if you faced each fear?

   ....

5. How would the hero in your story face these fears?

   ....

CHAPTER 5

Fuel Your Confidence

Confidence is like a muscle. The more you push yourself to take action, the more confidence you gain in your own skills and mindset. In the same way that muscles don't get stronger without exercise, your confidence won't grow unless you push yourself. There's no trick to it. You have to jump right in.

Once you start taking action, you'll start seeing signs of progress. This feeds your confidence. If you never attempt anything, you won't achieve progress, you won't see any evidence of success, and you'll never begin to learn what you're capable of.

Learning, after all, comes from trying new things. Even if

you try something and fail, you still learn from the experience, and that learning better prepares you for the next time you try something new. Even if you're successful only 50 percent of the time, that 50 percent demonstrates your skills and abilities, so you can build upon it. That's how confidence grows over time. As you become more confident in your abilities, you'll find it easier to confront bigger challenges. That's why confidence is a building block of courage.

It's similar to being an athlete. As a kid, a runner might dream about going to the Olympics, but if all she does is stare at herself in the mirror every day and say, "I'm an Olympian, I'm an Olympian," she will never achieve that dream. To get to the Olympics, that kid will have to go to the track every day and run, and keep running, getting better over time because she practices constantly. As she runs more, her performance will improve, and she will start to see evidence of success. In fact, every day she will be a little better than she was the day before until, eventually, she can run like a champion and compete at an international level.

A GENDER GAP IN CONFIDENCE

If lack of confidence is a problem for you, understand that it's a widespread problem, particularly for women.

Over the course of the many interviews I conducted for this book, I noticed a distinction between the men and women I talked to. Many of the successful women I talked to either seemed unaware of or were actively apologetic for their success. They didn't seem to think their success was praiseworthy. I found this remarkable because many of these women have done extraordinary things. Instead of focusing on how far they had come, they focused on how far they still needed to go. They built their drive and determination around their purpose. They lacked the same level of swagger that I observed in many of the successful men I interviewed.

THE WINNING WOMEN PROGRAM

In 2015, Ernst & Young named me one of their Entrepreneurial Winning Women—a distinction given to the top 1–2 percent of women entrepreneurs who have built outstanding, high-growth businesses. When I received the call, my first reaction was disbelief: "You must have the wrong number." I couldn't understand why I had received such an honor.

Ernst & Young conducts a thorough analysis for this award. They select a handful of women from thousands of applications. They evaluate the performance of their companies and examine a considerable amount of data, undertaking a significant assessment process to make their selection. I didn't win a popularity contest based on the votes of my peers. Ernst & Young objectively concluded from their research that I was a high-performing woman entrepreneur.

Nevertheless, I couldn't relate to it. I found it difficult to accept the recognition because of lingering self-doubt. Had there been some sort of mistake? What if I accepted the recognition only to find out later that they had read the data incorrectly or contacted the wrong person? It seemed like a possibility, and I knew the consequences would be embarrassing and devastating.

That level of self-doubt is not unique to me. I've found that many successful women struggle to be confident and acknowledge their achievements. This holds them back from dreaming even bigger and taking bigger risks, which ultimately hinders the level of success they achieve.

In fact, EY's Entrepreneurial Winning Women program was designed to empower women entrepreneurs to think bigger, gain access to capital, learn from their peers, and find seasoned advisors. These connections help their companies scale, increasing employment and prosperity.

My own participation in the program over the last couple

of years has dramatically shifted my thinking, boosted my confidence, and empowered a belief in myself. I no longer question whether or not I deserve recognition. I don't deny the level of success I have achieved. On the contrary, I fully accept that I have achieved great things, and this acceptance increases my confidence to dream even bigger, take more daring risks, and scale greater heights. Much of the success I now enjoy came about as a result of this shift in mindset and confidence.

HOW TO FUEL YOUR CONFIDENCE

Here's a five-question exercise that will lead you toward an actionable plan designed to fuel your confidence.

First, think about the dream you identified earlier. You addressed the fears associated with this dream in the previous chapter. Now it's time to become action oriented, to move from dreaming to doing. What are the top five priorities to achieve your dream? At the beginning of my entrepreneurial journey, my top five priorities included building a business, creating an education platform, becoming a public speaker, writing a book, and launching a nonprofit focused on public policy. Start broadly, examining the outcomes you need to achieve to reach your dream.

Next, home in on a more immediate horizon. What are the

top five priorities you must achieve this year? Take your list from question one and fixate on one or two of those items, setting goals to accomplish them by the end of the year. The overall priorities might not be met by then, but you can use these broad priorities to establish specific, related goals that are achievable. My top five annual priorities included completing the book, speaking every month, building partnerships with policymakers, expanding my business, and mastering one new skill.

From there, hone in even more. Examine the priorities from the previous step and find the top five priorities you could achieve this quarter. These will help you progress toward meeting the bigger annual goals. My top five quarterly priorities included developing the book concept, creating the book outline, interviewing successful people for research, documenting my framework, and understanding the needs of my audience.

Next, determine what actions you need to take to meet these quarterly priorities. For example, maybe your quarterly goal is to launch a podcast. To get there, some of the actions you would need to take include learning about your audience, connecting with them, doing the necessary research, writing the content, and preparing the platform. Personally, I needed to commit to writing every single day regardless of how I felt.

Finally, determine what metrics you will use to track your weekly progress. For example, in launching the podcast, you set a goal to focus on it one hour every day. You would then track your progress each week to see if you've met that goal. If not, then you know you must strive to improve your performance. For me, that means dedicating at least one hour every weekday and eight hours every weekend toward my priorities.

The more actions you take and track, the more your confidence will grow as you begin to see the connection between what you do on a daily basis and how that leads you toward your goals. From there, like a cascade, you begin to see progress toward your quarterly goals, your annual goals, and ultimately your long-term big dream.

However, sometimes we get lost in the details, and when that happens, we run the risk of becoming demoralized. Instead of simply creating lists of priorities, select a theme to guide you. The details matter, but you have to hold onto the big picture so you can regain your focus. This is one reason why companies have mission statements. After all, even a successful business can get lost in their annual, quarterly, and weekly goals. When this happens to you, a power word can get you back on track.

WHAT'S YOUR POWER WORD?

Every New Year's Eve, people make resolutions. They start off with big goals like losing weight, exercising daily, or achieving some other form of self-improvement. By March, most of those resolutions have been forgotten. Our dreams tend to be long term, so in order to get there, we must create a system of accountability. Progress must be tracked on a regular basis to maintain focus.

An effective way I've found to do that is to come up with a mantra or motto that keeps you on track. I prefer a single word because it's impossible to forget. Instead of making any resolutions, I pick one word that best describes the priorities I must achieve that year. In thinking about your top five priorities for the year, consider a theme that captures those priorities.

For example, if your priorities all relate to gaining a new skill, one word to encapsulate that might be "learning." Perhaps your five priorities relate to building a personal brand or becoming debt free. Your priorities should excite you, so find one word to remind you why you're excited. This will help keep you focused.

Your short-term priorities can change as you discover more efficient ways of achieving the same outcomes. However, if you stay true to your one word, your actions will still contribute to your overall dream.

A laundry list of resolutions and goals can easily be forgotten. Now you have to focus on only one word. Anytime your actions don't align with that word, just examine what you're doing. Then learn from that experience and get back on track.

MY WORD FOR 2017

As my business was growing, things started to feel chaotic and stressful. Suddenly, we had an overabundance of work. This was a natural result of exponential growth, but we found it hard to keep up with everything.

I realized that to scale intelligently, do right by our customers, and allow our team to thrive, we needed more discipline. We needed discipline in how we choose the clients we work with, how we choose the people we hire, how we do the work, how we scale, and how we produce results. Everything needed to become more consistent, so for 2017, the word I chose was "discipline."

Discipline mattered not just for my company but also for me personally. My health suffered from the sheer stress of my company's growth. Discipline forced me to create daily rituals that ensured I always focused on the right actions. I developed daily health habits, such as working out and eating at the right times. Maintaining a healthy lifestyle benefited both my team and me. At work, we developed rituals and practices in our company that gave us a healthier, more effective way to scale so we wouldn't burn ourselves out. It also gave us a regular cadence of how we measured our progress and adapted to change.

CONSISTENT ACTIONS BUILD CONFIDENCE

If you are sprinting toward your destination, you spend all of your energy quickly and give up. If you want long-term growth, you have to run a marathon. Adopting a marathon mindset requires discipline because you're setting a pace that you can maintain.

Confidence is the result of relentless action. If you want more confidence, take more action. Don't just think about it or wish for it or read a book about it. Do more. The more you do, the more you learn, and the more you learn, the more your confidence will develop to make you the courageous hero you are meant to be.

EXERCISE

1. What are the top five priorities to achieve your dream?

   ....

2. What are the top five priorities that you must achieve this year?

   ....

3. What are the top five priorities that you must achieve this quarter?

   ....

4. What are the consistent actions required to achieve your priorities?

   ....

5. What are the key metrics to track your progress?

   ....

CHAPTER 6

Flip Your Failure

Despite your dream and all of your well-constructed plans, one negative experience can tempt you to give up. Nobody enjoys failing, but if you spend all of your effort trying to avoid failure, you might just avoid success in the process. Keep taking risks, no matter what happens, because risks are necessary on the road to success.

FAILURE IS FEEDBACK

Reframe every failure as a learning opportunity. Think of your failure as feedback. It's a data point that tells you what doesn't work. It's a course of action you can cross off your list. Now you know what not to do, so you're free to try something different.

The faster you learn, the faster you can pivot toward success. Let's say you are presented with a decision that has eight different possible approaches. You try one, and it fails. That just means you now have seven options left. You try another one, and it fails. Now you have six to choose from. The more often you fail, the closer you get to the one thing that works because you're eliminating all of the things that don't.

One advantage of failure is that it produces a strong negative emotion, and negative emotions tend to create lasting memories. A painful enough experience will generate a lasting, impactful memory that you can learn from. As strange as it sounds, vividly remembering a negative experience is more beneficial than remembering a positive one. Why? Because you're more likely to retain what you learned from the experience and apply it to future actions, making success easier to achieve over time.

DEALING WITH CONSTANT FAILURE

My company, BeyondCurious, provides consulting services to large, multi-billion-dollar corporations. However, in the beginning, things were much different. When I was new in this business, I had no brand, no clients, no case studies, and almost no capital. That made it very difficult to gain the trust of large corporations.

Every day I reached out to numerous people, and every day I got rejected over and over again. However, through sheer persistence, I eventually had the opportunity to meet with executives from a major corporation. They invited my company to place a bid for some work, so we submitted a proposal. We made it all the way to the final round, but at that point, they told us our company was too small, too new in the marketplace.

My team and I felt dejected, but we didn't allow ourselves to give up. Eventually, they invited us to place another bid, but the same thing happened all over again. We made it to the final round, and they told us we were too small and too new.

FROM FAILURE TO SUCCESS

Each time we failed, I asked them for a follow-up meeting so I could obtain feedback. I wanted to learn from our failures. The first time we lost a bid was quite painful, but we felt far more resilient the second time. The third time, it didn't bother us at all. We kept at it. In fact, we failed eleven consecutive times, and after every failure, I asked for a follow-up meeting. Through those meetings, I learned what we could improve, as well as what we'd done right.

Each time, we applied what I'd learned. By the time we

reached the twelfth bid, we had narrowed the gap between their expectations and our solution, and finally, on that twelfth bid, we won. We've never looked back. This company was the first major client to hire us, and we've been extremely successful ever since.

That initial success gave us credibility in the marketplace. We grew exponentially as a result. None of our incredible success would have happened if we had given up after the first, second, or even the eleventh rejection.

INCREASE YOUR RATE OF FAILURE

Be clear about the outcome you desire. I knew we had to get a large company to hire us so that we could do great work and earn their advocacy. Earning their endorsement would put us on the map and give us credibility with other large corporations around the world.

I had connections to the right decision-makers there. I could see the pathway. If I'd given up, I would have closed the door to our best opportunity, so moving on never seemed like an option. Instead, I learned, adapted, and improved until I succeeded.

As long as you're clear about the outcome you want and why that outcome is important, you should never give up. Keep learning and improving and changing strategies until you achieve the outcome you want.

HOW CAN YOU FLIP YOUR FAILURES?

The series of questions in this exercise will help you flip your failures, turning them into learning opportunities that contribute to your long-term dream.

First, what is a failure you flourished from? Recall a time in your life when a failure led to some kind of personal growth, an instance where, afterward, you said, "I'm glad I failed because if I hadn't, I would not have learned a lesson that helped me succeed." Document this failure.

Second, what did you learn from the experience? Think about what this failure taught you. As you write it down, try to include details so you can see how much value you received from this failure.

Third, how did this failure motivate you? Determine why you kept trying, because in figuring that out, you will discover the driving force that keeps you going. Some motivation kept you resilient and made you tenacious after this failure because you kept striving. What was that motivation?

Finally, how did you grow as a result of this failure? Maybe it made you a better, stronger person. Maybe it taught you something that helped you later in life. Maybe it gave you enough clarity to make wiser decisions.

Of course, it's also important to consider the downsides to failing. How long did it take you to recover from this failure in your life? Maybe it took only a short amount of time to bounce back, or maybe it took far longer. If you've recovered and come out the other side, what drove that timeline? Did you hold onto the negative feelings? Could you have recovered faster if you'd dealt with the aftermath differently? How might you have benefited even more?

Often, after we've experienced a failure and come out the other side, we look back and wonder why we spent so much time moping about something we couldn't change instead of spending time recovering. This is certainly true in romantic relationships. People grieve their breakups, and later, after they've moved on to a better relationship, they wonder why they spent so much time mourning. Hopefully, with this exercise, you can flip your failures, learn from them, recover faster, and flourish.

HOW I FLIPPED MY FAILURES

At a certain point in my life, I felt thoroughly miserable about all of the setbacks I'd experienced and the hardships I'd gone through. However, when I reflected on my failures and mapped them out, I realized that every one of them had actually catapulted me to a better place. They made me stronger, wiser, and ultimately more successful.

This relates to the epiphany I had while playing the video game. In the game, failing actually helped me reach higher levels. When I failed, I adjusted my approach and kept taking action. With each failure, as long as I kept trying, I found myself able to get farther in the game. This caused my confidence to grow.

I lost multiple times at level one, but each time, I went back to the starting point and played again. Over time, I mastered the level and moved on to level two, repeating the process. Along the way, I realized that the faster I recovered from failure, the faster I got to the end of the level.

Think of it this way: When you start working out, you get fatigued quite easily, but over time, as you persevere and continue exercising on a regular basis, you get stronger. As you get stronger, you recover faster, and you find yourself able to lift heavier weights, run faster, and endure a longer exercise regimen. This becomes a cycle. You exercise, you become fatigued, you recover, you exercise again, you become stronger, and over time, your momentum speeds up.

Successful people take more chances. Sometime their failures aren't visible because they're so small, but they do fail. Even the most successful entrepreneurs experience regular failure and disappointment, but they try new things, never give up, and learn faster than anyone else. If you increase your rate of failure, you increase your rate of success. That's how it works, so long as you're willing to learn.

EXERCISE

1. What is a failure you flourished from?

   GRG imploding

2. What did you learn from the experience?

   Enjoyed working with small groups - leading + creating

3. How did this failure motivate you?

   Exciting raising $

4. How did you grow as a result of this failure?

   Know i can do it + try new things.

SECTION 3

CONVICTION

Conviction empowers you to stay the course, no matter what happens. When you fail or encounter hardship, it's natural to want to give up or find an easy way out. It's tempting to start thinking that the grass is greener somewhere else, but when you have conviction, you will persevere, no matter what barriers you encounter. If you give up at level one, you have no shot at level two, but if you stay the course, you will eventually overcome every obstacle in your way. Conviction stems from clarity and is fueled by courageous action. But to maintain your conviction in the long term, you must keep learning, adapting, and celebrating. Rona Kotecha's story gives us a perfect example.

RONA'S STORY

Rona's family lived in Uganda during the reign of the violent dictator Idi Amin. Three weeks after her birth, Rona's parents fled the country during the mass exodus that followed his rise to power. They settled in the United Kingdom and attempted to build a new life for themselves.

The town where Rona's family wound up was an industrial city in England. Her parents decided to start market trading, so they traveled to nearby villages and coastal towns to sell women's clothes. Because it was a family business, Rona began helping her parents, working in market stalls at the age of ten. She went to school during the week, but her evenings were spent purchasing goods with her parents, and her weekends were spent working in the market. On the weekends in particular, she worked very long hours. On Sunday, her workday typically started at 4 a.m. since they had a long journey to the coastal towns.

Rona got used to playing an active part in the family business. She not only helped her parents make ends meet, but she also helped her siblings with their homework. She learned early on the discipline of hard work and the value of time and money.

She had very little time to play, though it's doubtful she

would have done much playing even if she'd had the time. Through her family's struggles, Rona had developed a deep sense of responsibility. She knew what her parents had gone through to leave Uganda, how they'd arrived in the United Kingdom with almost nothing, and how hard they had worked to provide their children with a better future. Rona had learned that there's more to life than hanging out with friends and having fun.

Because of her deep sense of responsibility, she never felt burdened by working in the family business, taking care of her siblings, or helping with chores at home. She decided not to follow her friends to university so she could continue to support her family and look after the family business. She worked seven days a week, bouncing between the markets and a store the family acquired. In the process, she accrued valuable experience.

Living Core Values

In 1993, the family decided to move to Rwanda, where Rona's father, supported by her mother and sister, started a new business. Rona stayed behind in the United Kingdom, working while finishing her education part-time. In 1994, her family went through the terrible Rwandan genocide, losing absolutely everything they had worked so hard to build.

By this time, Idi Amin had been out of power in Uganda for many years, so the family returned to Uganda to start over yet again. Her father took out a loan to start a business there. Even though they still had very little, they remained resilient through the pain, loss, and changes. They even managed to help others in their community. All of this imparted to Rona the lessons of generosity, sharing, and humility.

Rona's brother Ashish decided to leave school at fifteen so he could support the family. He started a technology company, supporting the family business by helping Rona's father import goods into Africa. Rona moved to Dubai to support the growing family business. Though she didn't have the skills to master some of the tasks required in the expanding business, she taught herself everything she needed to know. Together with her siblings, she took the family business to the next level.

As the business grew, Rona took on greater and greater roles. Today, her family operates a multisector company in Africa, Mara Group, a pan-African business services company that has expanded into the Middle East.

Creating a Social Enterprise

After working in the Middle East for a few years, Rona

moved back to London, got married, and raised a family. Even then, her sense of responsibility and service led her to continue innovating. Rona's brother dreamed of finding ways to empower entrepreneurs and create change. That was the inspiration behind the Mara Foundation, which launched in 2009.

In 2012, Ashish asked Rona to lead the foundation and scale the Mara Mentor initiative. Despite being a mom to three-month-old twins and a two-and-a-half-year-old, Rona decided to accept the challenge. Mara Mentor, a social enterprise focused on mentoring emerging entrepreneurs to start up and scale their businesses, provides mentorship, resources, support, and tools to help entrepreneurs become successful.

In taking on these responsibilities, Rona went through an internal roller coaster. She worried that she was letting her kids down by spending so much time on her new endeavor. She wondered whether she could manage both a family and a growing business. Despite the difficulties, she never gave up. She developed confidence by continuing to take steps forward. She learned new skills and adapted to change in both the marketplace and her family's expectations.

Rona has made a profound impact on the lives of many

people, and she enjoys what she's doing. She has discovered that the secret to dealing with self-doubt lies in learning and growing. She has also become a wonderful role model for many people, including her own children. Her eldest, now eight, has asked if she can follow in her mother's footsteps of empowering others by joining the Mara Foundation.

Ultimately, Rona wanted to change the narrative of what's possible in people's lives because her family had survived so much. Though she ventured into areas she knew nothing about, she learned and adapted, driven by her deep sense of responsibility and service. Now she gets to celebrate the impact she is making in the lives of so many people.

The story doesn't end here, however. Rona dreams of expanding the reach of the Mara Foundation to millions of people globally. Hers is a story of conviction, of never giving up, no matter what challenges came her way.

GRIT IS THE SECRET TO SUCCESS

In interviewing hundreds of successful people, I found that they almost always credit grit and tenacity as key reasons why they have become successful. They might have failed many times, but they just didn't give up. Each time they failed, they learned new skills, changed their approach, tried new things, adapted, and got better. They kept going until they were successful.

Don't just stay the course and keep doing the same things that aren't working. Stay on the path, but keep trying new things and testing new approaches. Success is inevitable when you refuse to give up, treat failure as feedback, and keep learning and adapting until you get the desired outcome.

Staying the course can be very challenging, and you can keep going only if you refuel your enthusiasm by recognizing how far you've come and celebrating your successes. Otherwise, you will run out of steam and give up. Treat your journey like a marathon, and maintain your pace and energy.

NATASHA'S STORY

Natasha Case had a happy upbringing and received a stellar education. She also possessed a strong sense of ambition. During high school, she became interested in studying architecture because she thought it might create more career options. Since both of her parents worked in creative fields—animation and architecture—she felt inspired by them, but at the same time, she wanted to do things differently.

Despite wanting to assert her uniqueness, she became an architect at Walt Disney Imagineering, a literal hybrid of what her parents did. She worked in hotel and master planning for three months as a contractor in the hope of gaining full-time employment. However, just one month before being hired full-time, the recession hit, and Walt Disney Imagineering instituted a company-wide hiring freeze.

Natasha panicked. Her planned pathway blocked, she didn't know what to do next. She didn't have a concrete backup plan, only a quirky, passionate hobby she had been thinking about for years: an idea of merging food and design. Friends and colleagues suggested it was a good time for her to explore this idea, but to Natasha, it didn't seem like a viable option. Failing to get the Imagineering job was the first major setback she'd experienced in her life, so she didn't know how to navigate the resulting emotions.

Eventually, she got another job in the design field, doing sales and marketing for a design trade show, but the momentum for growth and a path for climbing the ladder at that company didn't exist. Instead, the job was little more than day-to-day work. Since she had nothing to lose at that point, she started to think seriously about her side hobby. Maybe it was time to give it a try and chase her dream.

When Your Path Closes, Find Another Path

Natasha had a passion for architecture, but she felt like it was a disconnected field, even though architects make a huge impact on society. In fact, architects design the urban landscapes around us. As she thought about this, Natasha realized that if she wanted to do something meaningful with her architectural knowledge, she would have to get creative, combining it with other interests and using those interests to make architecture more accessible.

She came up with a concept of using food to talk about design and called it farchitecture: food plus architecture. One of the first iterations of this concept was designing an ice cream sandwich inspired by architecture and naming it after famous designers. By combining her passion for design with her love of food, she created her innovative company, Coolhaus.

At the time, grocery stores didn't carry artisan ice cream brands. However, building a brick-and-mortar store wasn't an option for Natasha because she simply didn't have the money. She also didn't yet understand the wholesale space. All she had was a unique idea to make architecturally inspired ice cream sandwiches and the design skills to create the branding. Somehow, she had to launch this very boutique concept in a category dominated by big brands and cookie-cutter products.

Creative Bootstrapping Pays Off

She decided to use a food truck to sell her ice cream. Since there were no other LA-based gourmet ice cream products like hers, she had to figure out a creative way to promote her company. She decided that a great place to launch would be the Coachella Music Festival.

Unfortunately, Natasha couldn't figure out how to get there. She had spent all of her money on the truck—an old, refurbished mail delivery truck. It couldn't even drive down the street, much less get her all the way from Los Angeles to Coachella. She learned that if she joined AAA Platinum, she would receive one free 200-mile tow. That was just far enough to get her to the desert where Coachella took place, so on the morning of Coachella, she pretended the truck broke down, even though it had never worked in the first place. The truck got towed out into the desert in time for the launch. The moral of the story? Creative bootstrapping pays off.

Natasha debuted her ice cream at the festival, using the truck as a prop and utilizing social media to promote the idea of gourmet ice cream as a mobile food. The idea took off and instantly became viral.

While this initial experience proved successful, it was only the beginning of a long, arduous journey. Nevertheless, from that point on, Natasha had a clear purpose to become a game changer and innovator. She wanted to do something radically different. Her big dream for Coolhaus was to become a household brand, the Ben & Jerry's of the millennial generation.

Based on her success at Coachella, Natasha purchased more food trucks to sell the product at various locations. New challenges arose with this expansion. Now that she was selling ice cream in different cities, she had to figure out how to maintain consistent quality and service, and she had to deal with the logistical challenges of running a business that was so difficult to scale.

Keep Pivoting Closer to Success

The strain started to affect Natasha's business, so she decided to revisit the sales channels that hadn't been possible in the beginning: wholesale and brick-and-mortar. She looked for good brick-and-mortar locations and also reached out to Whole Foods to do a local test of five ice cream sandwich SKUs (stock-keeping units). Very quickly, though, Natasha saw that they were going to need real investment to make either of those options succeed.

Even though her company was composed primarily of food trucks, massive buzz was generated around the brand. That buzz, combined with the rapid growth of Coolhaus, piqued the interest of investors. Natasha received her first angel round of funding. Although it was not a massive success, the right timing and the right investors helped her business grow exponentially. The secret sauce? Concentrating on wholesale. It was scalable with low overhead, and it provided an option for exiting. Coolhaus now doubles and triples wholesale every year, and they continue to produce the highest-quality product while pushing through barriers to expand their reach.

Throughout her journey, Natasha evolved as a leader, a business owner, and an entrepreneur. She knew this was more than just a hobby. She had to master not only the creative side of designing a product but also the business side of making it profitable and achieving growth.

To do that, she had to learn new skills, take risks, and fail many times. Because of her willingness to do that, she eventually found the right people, manufacturers, and investors to make her business successful. Looking at her success now, people would have no idea how many times she had to cold-call potential investors and retailers, begging them to take a chance on her. So much of her journey to this point has been messy and painful, but she has persevered.

What drove her, despite every hardship, was her conviction that Coolhaus could become this generation's Ben & Jerry's, her desire to become a game changer, and her passion for innovation. She stayed focused, and as a result, she now gets to celebrate her huge success as a highly recognized company in her market.

THREE STEPS TO BUILDING CONVICTION

Conviction is strengthened by learning, adapting, and celebrating.

Learning helps you gain the skills and confidence to feel a sense of progress. You learn through hardship. You learn through failures. You even learn from other people and their journeys, recognizing in their experiences the attitudes and behaviors you need to adopt. Learning helps you discover new solutions and empowers you to keep going instead of giving up.

Adapting to change helps you stay the course. The women in these stories kept trying new things. When one pathway closed, they looked for another way forward. When they failed at something, they looked for another way to succeed. They didn't let anything deter them from reaching their goals.

Celebration refuels you for what's ahead while acknowledging your progress in the journey, but celebration isn't just about rewards and recognition. It's about gratitude for what you have, and hope and optimism for the future.

CHAPTER 7

Keep Learning

Learning begins with curiosity—a gift we're all born with. As children, we are incredibly curious as we explore, create, learn, and play. However, as we get older, we tend to lose that innate sense of curiosity and playfulness. We grow comfortable with how much we already know instead of letting our childlike curiosity take us into a wonderland of discovery. Let learning be an adventure with endless possibilities. The things you'll discover and experience will make the exploration worthwhile, especially as you pursue your big dream.

Dig deeper. If you're curious about something, don't just satisfy your curiosity with the first book you read on the topic. Read more. Learn from multiple sources. Let your curiosity guide you. After all, that's what kids do. The first satisfactory answer to a compelling question doesn't end their curiosity. If anything, they become even more obsessed with it.

If you want better outcomes, ask better questions. When your questions are powerful, your creativity is unleashed and your learning is accelerated. Don't let your insecurity of not knowing the answer prevent you from asking questions. Great questions give you insights and perspectives to overcome seemingly insurmountable challenges.

Avoid arrogance about your current level of understanding. If you're convinced that you know all you need to know, you will create a barrier to learning. Instead, remain open and humble, welcoming new ideas and perspectives. You will gain insights you never imagined, becoming a sponge that soaks up knowledge from the people around you.

No matter what challenge you're currently dealing with, learning can help you overcome it. In a video game, you might fail multiple times when trying to get past a certain obstacle, but if you keep at it, learning will help you discover new solutions to eventually overcome that obstacle. Learning gets you to the next level.

Become a continuous learner, and you will overcome every

barrier standing in your way. You will discover things you didn't know, and that, in turn, will make you hungry for more.

WHAT CAN HELP YOU KEEP LEARNING?

The five questions in this exercise are designed to help you adopt and maintain an attitude of constant learning.

First, what are the gaps you have today in terms of realizing your big dream? What do you lack in knowledge or skills that you need to make your dream come true? If you dream of starting a business, perhaps you know how to create the product, but you lack knowledge on managing the financial and legal aspects of a business. To spread ideas and reach my audience, I needed to be a highly effective public speaker. However, I struggled with stage fright, unable to communicate in a public setting.

Second, after you have identified the gaps, what are some ways you could fill them? Maybe you could take a class. Maybe you could read a book or watch a video. Maybe you need someone to help you get started, like a mentor, consultant, or business partner. There are so many different ways to fill in the gaps to reach your goals; you just have to get creative to find them.

Third, what will help you fill those gaps faster, better, and more effectively? You have a list of options, but now you need to think about which ones provide exponentially faster results. Narrow down your list to focus on solutions that bring the most success. Reflect on your performance and get tips from pros.

Fourth, once you have figured out which solutions are most effective, what do you need to do each week to close the gaps? Create a list of simple tasks that will be easy to track. For example, maybe you can set a goal to read something about the topic every week. Maybe you can commit to keeping in touch with a mentor or coach on a regular basis. Find some way to make measurable weekly progress. When I needed to learn public speaking, I spent an hour each week practicing.

Finally, how will you measure your progress? You won't know how far you've come if you don't measure it. Your metrics reveal how you are doing, how much progress you've made toward your goal, and where you need to improve. It's not enough to merely identify the gaps and reveal what knowledge you need to acquire or what skills you must master. You also need to systematically track your progress every week so you can see the gaps closing and gain a sense of progress toward your ultimate goal.

COMMIT TO YOUR GROWTH PLAN

Speaking in front of others, even a small crowd, terrified me. I suffered from severe stage fright. I had no confidence as a speaker, even though I had absolute belief in the message I wanted to share. I asked myself if I was willing to let my fear be greater than my desire to create impact. I realized that the worst-case scenario was embarrassing myself, but the best case was inspiring someone to believe in themselves. Public speaking provided me with a platform to make a real difference. I did not want to let my fear hold me back, so I committed to mastering this skill.

I explored different ways to improve my public speaking skills. I watched videos of renowned speakers, read books on the topic, took some training courses, and even got advice from successful public speakers. I tried a variety of approaches to figure out what helped me learn most effectively.

Ultimately, I discovered that the fastest and most effective way to close the gap was to simply do it. I could read every book on the shelf, watch every video online, and attend every training program, but unless I got up on a stage and spoke, I would never master public speaking. It turns out that there's no better way to become an eloquent public speaker than to speak in public frequently.

I made a commitment to speak at least once a month, even if it was in front of a tiny audience. Though at times I was ineffective, and even occasionally terrible, I became more comfortable speaking in front of people. I developed techniques for overcoming stage fright and anxiety. I learned to focus on the needs and interests of my audience instead of worrying about myself. As I kept practicing and speaking, my competence level increased, and I learned how to express myself more clearly, how to gain and keep an audience's attention, and how to deliver extraordinary value every single time.

I tracked my monthly speaking engagements, measured my progress, and continued to learn from other public speakers. Eventually, I gained a competency level that placed me in a position to be an established public speaker at events around the world. Above all, I embraced my authenticity and found my own voice.

My experience taught me that whatever you want to achieve, you can get there if you remain curious, open, and committed. Learning fuels our confidence, helps elevate us to higher levels, and gives us the strength to persist through challenges.

EXERCISE

1. What are the gaps in your ability to realize your dream?

    ....

2. What are all of the ways to close these gaps?

    ....

3. What will help you get results faster, better, and more effectively?

    ....

4. What do you need to do each week to close the gap?

    ....

5. How will you measure your progress?

    ....

CHAPTER 8

Keep Adapting

Our survival depends on our ability to adapt, because no matter how much we plan or anticipate, things inevitably change. Success does not come from repeating what's not working regardless of circumstances. To reach our goals, we must be willing to adapt our approach. The faster and more agile you are in adapting, the greater your effectiveness and chance of success.

ADAPTING TO DISRUPTION

If we don't adapt, we perish. As the pace of change accelerates, we are thrown into an environment of chaos and uncertainty. Large corporations provide thousands of jobs and often become the pillars of the communities in which they operate. Yet every year, many well-known corporations go out of business and disappear completely, simply because they failed to adapt to change. Jobs are lost, families are impacted, and local economies are destroyed as a consequence.

Change is inherently difficult, but it is also the source of innovation and transformation. When we adapt to change, we gain the opportunity to transform ourselves to reach a higher level of success. And when the world as we know it gets disrupted, we have the responsibility and privilege of defining what comes next. After all, when things fall apart, it's time to build something even more purposeful and profound.

Adapting requires changing the way you've always done things, stepping out of your comfort zone, developing new skills, changing your mindset, and going boldly into new, unfamiliar territory. Change can feel uncomfortable because it takes us into the unknown. As we leave the familiar behind, we don't know for sure where we'll wind up, and that can be scary. Doing this incrementally can help ease the difficulty of the process, allowing us to adapt more easily.

HOW TO KEEP ADAPTING

These six questions will help you break down a giant

change into manageable chunks to make adapting easier. You'll notice your progress more and track it better when you focus on accomplishing small tasks on a weekly basis, rather than attempting to tackle one big goal that might take months.

First, what were your priorities last week? We talked about the importance of setting weekly priorities in order to work in a measurable way toward your long-term goals. The purpose of setting those smaller goals was to make the necessary changes more comfortable by making them incremental.

Second, what did you achieve in regard to your priorities last week? Identify your successes against your goals. Were you able to achieve all of the goals you set for yourself? What helped you get there?

Third, what are some areas in which you got stuck while trying to focus on your priorities? List the things that got in your way or slowed your progress. This will help you identify patterns in your skillset or mindset, and then identify ways to overcome these barriers.

Fourth, what do you need to do differently this week to avoid getting stuck again? Think about some other strategies you can adopt to work more effectively on your priorities. If you aren't achieving the goals you set, you don't have to change the goals. Just change your strategy.

Fifth, what did you learn last week? Just as we're always changing, whether we realize it or not, we are always learning. Often, we fail to document what we learn, so we might not even realize how much progress we've made and how much we've grown.

Finally, what are your priorities for next week? Documenting them allows you to stay on track to achieve your big dream. You want to work toward monthly, quarterly, and yearly progress, of course, but documenting your weekly progress is crucial to making the long-term goals achievable. You're not simply writing a to-do list. You are writing down the outcomes you want to create and what you need to do to get there.

By answering these questions, you give yourself a chance to reflect on the progress you've made so you can ensure it aligns with your priorities. We often reflect on failures, but with this exercise, you're reframing your mindset. You're thinking about how to do more of what's working, and how to navigate effectively through what's not working. Instead of getting paralyzed by the lack of progress, you're focusing on strategies to get unstuck. You're examining what you have learned so you can become better at the skills you possess while also developing new skills. This helps you determine what will keep you moving in the right direction.

REVIEW YOUR VISION AND ADAPT

The exercise you've just completed is something I've done for years. Every week, I sit down and review my vision, and I reflect on my yearly, quarterly, and monthly goals. This takes me just fifteen minutes but keeps me focused on what matters for the long haul. It helps me align my actions to my vision.

I look at my top five priorities for achieving my dream, then I answer those six questions. What were my priorities last week? What did I achieve? Where did I get stuck? What do I need to do differently next week to avoid getting stuck? What did I learn that can help me in the future? What are my priorities for the following week?

By doing this consistently, I create a catalog that enables me to see how far I've come. Seeing a written list of the things I have achieved gives me a clear sense of my progress, and it also feels tremendously fulfilling.

It's quite different from simply creating a checklist of tasks and working my way through it. When you do that, by the end of the week, you mostly just feel exhausted from getting things done. Instead, this approach is meant to keep you focused on the strategies that lead to real results and help you adapt quickly to change so you can move powerfully toward your vision.

SEEK PROGRESS OVER PERFECTION

With my company, BeyondCurious, I face so many challenges in growing my business and remaining innovative that I can become overwhelmed trying to determine the best way to lead. There are a million different things I could focus on. If I create a game plan at the start of the year and keep doing that without pivoting, we might wind up in the wrong place by the end of the year.

To keep the company innovative, I must identify our priorities and create a long-term vision. I take that long-term vision and translate it into three-year targets. From those three-year targets, I create one-year targets, and then I break those down into quarterly and weekly priorities. Throughout this process, I continually ask myself, "What are the most important things that need to get done? Are we achieving them? What do we need to do differently in the week ahead?"

That clarity allows me to lead my team more effectively,

adapting as necessary to keep making progress. After all, if we remain unchanging, all of our efforts will be wasted because we won't adapt to the marketplace. I go through this exercise every week, identifying our priorities in order to make sure we are working toward them. That helps us avoid getting stuck.

My weekly ritual has proved to be a powerful tool to maintain my conviction. Some weeks are successful; some are disastrous. Sometimes, I get distracted or discouraged, but my practice of weekly reflection and review keeps me going. It allows me to adapt to my circumstances, environment, and changing needs. The combination of consistency and self-reflection has produced the most significant shifts in my personal and professional life.

EXERCISE

1. What were your priorities last week?

....

2. What did you achieve in regard to your priorities last week?

....

3. What are some areas in which you got stuck while pursuing your priorities?

....

4. What do you need to do differently this week to avoid getting stuck again?

....

5. What did you learn last week?

....

CHAPTER 9

Keep Celebrating

Big dreams are not achieved in an instant. It takes years of hustle and grit to become an "overnight" success story, but it can be challenging to stay focused and motivated if you have no clear sense of progress or achievement along the way.

Celebrating plays a vital role in helping you maintain your conviction. At the onset of a big dream, you may feel tremendous enthusiasm and excitement to get started—then you actually get started. You might have some initial success, but eventually barriers and obstacles get in the way.

As soon as this happens, your energy and motivation might dwindle, and your conviction gets severely tested. An effective way to overcome this challenge is to reflect on how far you've come and how much you've learned. Acknowledge all of this and celebrate it. Celebration gives you the energy and motivation to keep going. Besides, you deserve it. You dreamed big, worked hard, and took huge risks.

CELEBRATE EVERY LITTLE VICTORY

If you've ever tried to lose weight, you know some weeks can be incredibly discouraging. Inevitably, even if you stick to your diet, there are certain weeks where you hit a plateau or, even worse, where you somehow gain back a few pounds. Those experiences can feel very discouraging, and they might tempt you to give up on your diet.

If you have a big goal, like fifty pounds, then a bad week can make that goal seem even more impossible. However, if you break down your goal into manageable pieces—a pound a week—you are much more likely to achieve these milestones, and you get to celebrate every little victory. Whenever you reach one of these small goals, you gain a sense of progress, which makes the discouraging weeks feel less overwhelming. This gives you constant fuel to keep going.

Do you make resolutions every year, try to keep them, and ultimately give up before the year is over, only to try again the following year? You're not alone. We've all been there. We often overestimate what we can accomplish in a year, which is why New Year's resolutions are often too lofty and destined to be abandoned.

At the start of the year, we are filled with optimism and set big goals, like losing all excess body weight or becoming totally debt free. We expect to achieve perfect results in a year when, in reality, it might take us much longer. On the other hand, we underestimate what is possible in a decade and therefore don't take a long-term view that can propel us forward.

Instead of getting stuck in this cycle, you will benefit from shifting your vision both farther into the future and closer at the same time. By giving yourself a longer period of time to reach your big goal—a few years, a decade—and tracking the short-term priorities necessary to get there, you will begin to see results surprisingly fast.

Consistency in the journey is key. Avoid obsessing about the end goal. Celebrate every milestone along the way. Recognize your progress so you have the enthusiasm to stay on course. The more frequent the milestones, the greater the effect—you become a champion who's constantly moving forward. When we take a long-term view of our goals and are consistent in our actions, we create extraordinary impact.

WHAT CAN HELP YOU KEEP CELEBRATING?

If you have difficulty celebrating your own accomplishments, answering these five questions should help.

First, what have been your biggest successes to date? No matter what you've gone through lately or how discouraged you might be, you have achieved something along the way. Take a moment to examine your achievements, especially the ones that were most impactful or that you feel proudest of.

Second, what are you grateful for? Identify all of the ways in which you've been blessed, no matter how small. Your attitude is the difference between feeling exhausted and feeling excited.

Third, what are some milestones you can create for your journey? Maybe you have a big vision you want to map out for the next five years. What can be your stepping-stones along the way? What quarterly, monthly, or weekly goals can you celebrate?

Fourth, who are the cheerleaders supporting you on your journey? They might be family members, friends, peers, mentors, or anyone else who champions you. Surround yourself with these people because their encouragement and support will help you stay on track.

Fifth, what are some ways you could celebrate hitting your milestones? Paint a vivid picture of your celebration. You might consider making these celebrations a regular event. Create a rewards program designed just for you and redeem a reward when you hit a milestone. This gives you something to look forward to in the short term as you strive for the long-term reward of realizing your big dream.

HOW I CELEBRATE MYSELF

Celebrating has helped me remain committed to my dreams. I use a dream journal to catalog the impact I've created, the ways in which I've helped people, and the goals I've achieved. I keep all of this in one place so I can look back periodically and reflect, especially in moments of failure, despair, and hardship. When I peruse my journal, I am reminded of just how far I've come and how much I've already accomplished.

I also use my journal to express gratitude for everything in my life. When we lead with gratitude, we are much more likely to have a positive perspective on the future. We feel lucky and make decisions with greater confidence and optimism. We appreciate the challenges, not just the opportunities. Instead of feeling scarcity and constant struggle, we experience a sense of abundance and success. Gratitude is a game changer!

My journal also serves as my personal rewards program catalog. I make a list of the ways in which I want to celebrate whenever I reach a milestone. It might be something small, like treating myself to a day at the spa, or it might be a bigger reward, like a vacation. Sometimes the reward is as simple as giving myself the time and space to do absolutely nothing for a few hours or a day. Celebration has helped me refuel myself, regain energy, and rekindle my motivation to dream even bigger.

Giving yourself time to pause and reflect is vitally important, especially when you reach those milestones. Otherwise, you can get caught up in the doing, chasing, giving, and running, and you'll get worn down. If you don't take the time to pause and reflect on how far you've come, exhaustion will catch up to you.

You have to celebrate how far you've come so you can gain a bolder perspective on how far you will get tomorrow. Think about how you've changed, learned, and grown. Imagine how much more you will change, learn, and grow in the years to come. Celebrate every little accomplishment, because you've worked hard, taken the risks, confronted your fears, and learned from your failures. You've earned it.

EXERCISE

1. What have been your biggest successes to date?

    ....

2. What are you grateful for?

    ....

3. What are some milestones you can create for your
    journey?

    ....

4. Who are the cheerleaders supporting you on your
    journey?

    ....

5. What are some ways you could celebrate hitting your
    milestones?

    ....

Conclusion

GOING BEYOND YOUR BARRIERS

We all start at level one, and we all have a timer that's counting down to zero. To advance to the next level, we have to gain clarity about what we want and why it matters. We must find the courage to face our fears and take action, and we must maintain the conviction to constantly move forward. Only then can we overcome the barriers and reach higher levels than we ever thought possible.

My parting words for you on your journey are to follow this framework for gaining clarity, becoming courageous, and holding onto your conviction. If you find yourself dreaming without moving forward, examine which of these three areas you are stuck in.

Do you have a big dream, but you're not clear about why it matters? Are you clear about why it matters, but you're struggling with fear? Has an experience with failure made you want to give up? Are you running out of steam and don't know how to keep going? Determine where you're struggling so you can work through the struggle method-ically and take steps to overcome it.

IT'S TIME TO UNLOCK YOUR LIMITLESS POTENTIAL

Answer the questions in this book to help you create your game plan. Share your big dream with others to stay accountable on your journey. Seek advice and support from your community, and find way to celebrate your achievements. Dare to believe in your dream, and start taking steps in that direction. Dream big, be bold, and unlock your limitless potential.

About the Author

Nikki Barua is a change agent with a big mission to unlock people's potential through ideas, inspiration, and tools for transformation. She is a successful entrepreneur, speaker and advisor who helps business leaders gain clarity of purpose and certainty of outcomes as they lead their organizations through change. She is the CEO of BeyondCurious, an award-winning digital transformation consultancy that partners with large companies to unlock innovation and growth. Barua has been recognized as a top female entrepreneur and has been featured in national media including Fortune and Forbes.

Made in the USA
San Bernardino, CA
06 May 2018